HOW TO HAVE peace *When* YOU'RE FALLING *to* PIECES

HOW TO HAVE peace

When YOU'RE FALLING *to* PIECES

rebecca rode

CFI
AN IMPRINT OF CEDAR FORT, INC.
SPRINGVILLE, UTAH

ISBN 13: 978-1-4621-1170-1

Published by CFI, an imprint of Cedar Fort, Inc., 2373 W. 700 S., Springville, UT 84663
Distributed by Cedar Fort, Inc., www.cedarfort.com

LIBRARY OF CONGRESS CATALOGING-IN-PUBLICATION DATA

Rode, Rebecca, 1981- author.
How to have peace when you're falling to pieces / Rebecca Rode.
pages cm
ISBN 978-1-4621-1170-1
1. Motherhood--Religious aspects--Church of Jesus Christ of Latter-day Saints. 2. Peace of mind--Religious aspects--Church of Jesus Christ of Latter-day Saints. 3. Church of Jesus Christ of Latter-day Saints--Doctrines. 4. Christian life--Mormon authors. I. Title.
BX8643.W66R63 2013
248.8'431--dc23

2012048503

Cover design by Angela D. Olsen
Cover design © 2013 by Lyle Mortimer
Edited and typeset by Michelle Stoll

Printed in the United States of America

10 9 8 7 6 5 4 3 2 1

For my incredible husband and children, for teaching me how to love. And for my mom, for her quiet example of joyful motherhood.

Acknowledgments

EVERY BOOK IS THE PRODUCT OF MANY WONDERFUL PEOPLE. I appreciate my beta readers, Jill Myler, Natalie Roberts, Maurine Walker, and Rachel Layton, who dropped everything for a while to scour my book. I'd also like to thank my critique group friends who gently guided me in the right direction: Adrienne, Roxy, Ruth, Karen, Karyn, Kaye, Pam, Scott, Zach, and Sarah. I'd like to thank the talented team at Cedar Fort who have been so helpful, including Michelle, Angela, Jennifer, Josh, Catherine, and Rodney.

And last, but not least, a special thank-you to my amazing husband and eternal companion, without whom I would have ended up in a straitjacket long ago.

Contents

Preface

"Would you just give me some peace!"

It's the silent—or not so silent—declaration of every mother.

Remember when our idea of finding peace included candlelit massage tables and quiet meditation? Now our idea of finding peace is probably three hours of sleep at a time or *not* being followed to the bathroom, just once.

The ideal and the reality of motherhood can be as different as Hawaii and Alaska. I realized this soon after my daughter was born. To be fair, my pre-baby expectations may have been a bit unrealistic. Within months of our marriage, I had wanted a baby. I'd seen young mothers with their sweet sleeping infants in car seats, all snuggled up in soft, homemade quilts and sighing as if they didn't have a care in the world. It seemed so effortless. How I longed to be a mother!

Now don't misunderstand. Much of that dream has come true. My three children are the joys of my life. A wise woman once said, "Making the decision to have a child—it's wondrous. It is to decide forever to have your heart go walking around outside your body."[1] That part is absolutely true.

But children change everything. Suddenly your needs and wants don't count anymore. Soon it doesn't matter if you are exhausted beyond all reason and it's only 9:30 a.m. or that you have a headache the size of Texas. And once they start actually interacting with the outside world, watch out! You are not only a house cleaner, a nutritionist, a nurse, and on-demand entertainment, but a chauffeur as well. And guess what—you have to do it all at once.

Mothers don't get any peace. There is no "pause" button on the mom remote. We don't get sick days. We plug on, day after day, trying desperately to shove thirty-six hours' worth of activities into our allotted twenty-four. And at the height of our stress, we are also expected to find peace.

Is it possible? Yes.

Is it easy? No.

This book was conceived from a near nervous breakdown. With three children under age six, a new house, an extended-family crisis, and crippling depression, I was completely overwhelmed. Having peace in my life sounded as likely as becoming captain of the USS *Enterprise*. Yet a bit of stillness of soul was exactly what I needed, so I went to the library. There were a dozen books on finding peace in general, and even more books on parenting techniques, but they weren't quite right. I wanted to know that I wasn't alone in my struggles. I wanted fun stories and short chapters. I wanted to know specifics about surviving tough times and tough kids with a touch of humor. Thus *How to Have Peace When You're Falling to Pieces* was born: a light read *by* a mother *for* other mothers who may need a little peace as much as I did.

Let's be fair, though. Those parenting books in the library, written by scientific experts or mothers with very large families, can be helpful. But this isn't a parenting book; rather, it's a book that celebrates mothers—those with twenty children or two; empty nesters or brand-new moms; single, divorced, working, or at-home moms. Our families are all different in size and circumstance. But we share one remarkable struggle: the desire for inner peace.

Peace in Pieces

Some of my most cherished memories are teaching my kids how to assemble puzzles. It can be very fulfilling. You start out with a seemingly impossible pile of pieces. You know that the pieces will eventually become a picture, and you even have the picture on the box to serve as a guide. But it can still seem daunting at first. As you take your time choosing the needed pieces and assembling it carefully, the puzzle eventually takes shape and becomes a picture.

Motherhood also has its pieces. Each of us has dozens of roles: "owie"-kisser, loving wife, toilet-cleaner, car-washer, weed-puller, laundry specialist, hair stylist, and more. In this book we will take some of the main elements that make a mother and piece them together. By the end of the book, we will have a broadened perspective of a "put together" mother (pardon the pun). And hopefully we'll have a few laughs along the way.

Finding peace as a mom is hard. The demands of our children's school and sports—mixed with household maintenance, meals, church requirements, and simply being a mom and a wife—can make us feel scattered. We may not be able to control everything in our lives. (In fact, let's be honest here: when do we ever have control over our lives?) But we can learn how to take control of the things we can, let the rest go, and enjoy doing it. We will explore mom guilt; perfectionism; overcoming clutter, stress, and depression; how to be a "fun" family; and more—but in short segments that even the busiest of moms can enjoy. This book is packed with funny and uplifting stories—hey, moms deserve fun stories too—as well as poems, scriptures, and great quotes from General Authorities who have already traveled the road of parenthood.

Let's go find some peace!

Notes

1. Elizabeth Stone, as quoted by Hillary Rodham Clinton, *It Takes a Village* (New York: Simon & Schuster, 1996), 7–8.

Puzzle Piece #1

Mother of Purpose

A mother of purpose recognizes her own worth. While she is continually reaching for higher ground, she also places realistic expectations on herself and allows herself satisfaction when attaining them. She acknowledges the need for divine help in her mothering role. A purposeful mother sheds the unnecessary elements of life that drag her down. She avoids spreading herself too thin by focusing on the most rewarding activities. Most importantly, she remembers that she is in a partnership with God Himself in raising His children.

1

Because She Is a Mother

"She broke the bread into two fragments and gave them to her children, who ate with eagerness. 'She hath kept none for herself,' grumbled the sergeant.
"'Because she is not hungry,' said a soldier.
"'No,' said the sergeant, 'because she is a mother.'"[1]

WHEN MANY OF MY FRIENDS WERE GRADUATING FROM COLlege or getting married, I lived in Romania. It was technically an orphanage-volunteer program for career experience and university credits. But above all, it was my first real introduction to motherhood. I fell head-over-heels in love with "my" special needs children, none of whom could even speak two words, but all of whom had an incredible capacity for love.

Their childhood was shockingly different from my own. These orphans, with mental and physical disabilities, were hidden from society. They spent almost every moment of their young lives in three rooms of a cold concrete building. Since diapers were so expensive, the children instead wore bunched-up pieces of clothing held up with plastic bags. I often saw a child wear a red shirt "diaper" one day and then wear it as a shirt the next.

One little girl, age four but the size of a nine-month-old, sat tied to a high chair all day. Her eyes were flat, her head hanging forward and drool dripping from her open lips. The workers thought she was deaf and blind because she had never spoken a word or even responded to them. I ached for that girl. I began talking and singing to her, feeding her, and stroking her back. It took the entire semester, but by the end she was looking around the room, laughing, babbling, and clapping her hands. The deadness in her eyes had been replaced with joy and purpose. I felt that nothing in the world could be more important than that little girl's happiness right then. My existence, my entire purpose, was wrapped up in her triumph. I felt desperately needed and whole for the first time in my life. I wondered if that was what it meant to be a mother.

I returned home the week before Christmas. That Sunday, the children in my ward got up to sing to their families in sacrament meeting. They were *beautiful.* Their hair was perfectly set, their clothes were neat and colorful, their smiles were full of excitement, and they walked and sang effortlessly. I started to blink away the tears.

At that moment, I promised myself that I would make a difference in the world. All children deserved to be that happy. I couldn't legally adopt "my" Romanian children, and I probably couldn't change their government or its laws, but somehow I would make the world a little better for my being here.

Mothers Can Change the World

In the years after that promise, I felt frustrated. Nothing had changed for "my" kids overseas. I had done some writing about them to spread awareness and had won some awards, but nothing had really changed. Their government and the adoption laws were virtually the same. It was unlikely that my orphans had the families and medical care they needed. I wondered if my service had done any lasting good at all.

It wasn't until I got married and had my own children that I finally understood the Lord's plan for me. My service wasn't really about those sweet orphan children, even though my work may have lifted their cares for a few short months. The service was for me. It was my own personal introduction to the most important work I would ever be blessed to perform—motherhood.

Mothers have a lot more power than we realize. The poet William Ross Wallace said, "The hand that rocks the cradle is the hand that rocks the world."[2] And Elder Neal A. Maxwell said, "When the real history of mankind is fully disclosed, will it feature the echoes of gunfire or the shaping sound of lullabies? . . . Will what happened in cradles and kitchens prove to be more controlling than what happened in congresses?"[3]

Mothers really can change the world. It certainly was true for the families of the stripling warriors (Alma 56:46–56). It was also true for George Washington, who said, "All I am I owe to my mother."[4] A mom's influence is incalculable and infinite, as it extends for decades and generations across time and into eternity.

> My existence, my entire purpose, was wrapped up in her triumph. I felt desperately needed and whole for the first time in my life. I wondered if that was what it meant to be a mother.

It has been nine years since my promise in sacrament meeting. Today, three of those beautiful, skipping primary children are my own. I haven't run for government office or made a blockbuster movie, but I am still changing the world. Every morning that I send my smiling children off with clean faces and a determination to choose the right, I am making a difference. My four year-old may not become president of the United States. He may not even become a senator. (I suppose I'll settle for a lawyer.) But as I watch my kids find their identities and start their own ripple of influence, I realize that my work is much more than satisfying physical needs. The difference I'm making in the world isn't a drastic overhaul. But it is a gentle shaping of my own little corner of it.

The Expectations of Motherhood

It's so easy to forget how meaningful our job really is. We just get caught up in the craziness of life, and before we know it, years have passed. We know motherhood is important, but there are other important things out there too. We have more options and devices and activities than any other generation. We also have a higher standard because of it—complete with frequent reminders of where we have fallen short.

Elder Jeffrey R. Holland spoke of a letter he received from an overwhelmed mother:

> Her anxiety tended to come on three fronts. One was that whenever she heard talks on LDS motherhood, she worried because she felt she didn't measure up or somehow wasn't going to be equal to the task. Secondly, she felt like the world expected her to teach her children reading, writing, interior design, Latin, calculus, and the Internet—all before the baby said something terribly ordinary, like "goo goo." Thirdly, she often felt people were sometimes patronizing, almost always without meaning to be, because the advice she got or even the compliments she received seemed to reflect nothing of the mental investment, the spiritual and emotional exertion, the long-night, long-day, stretched-to-the-limit demands that sometimes are required in trying to be and wanting to be the mother God hopes she will be.[5]

Isn't that interesting? Much of the crippling pressure we find ourselves under is from our assumptions about the world's expectations. I want to meet that woman and tell her she isn't alone. The better I get to know other women, the more I realize that most of us feel the same way. We understand each other's struggles because we are also traveling that difficult path. (I think it can be found on the corner of "Unrealistic Expectations Blvd." and "Under-appreciation Drive.")

Let's find out how that dear sister overcame her anxiety. Elder Holland continued:

> But one thing, she said, keeps her going: "Through the thick and the thin of this, and through the occasional tears of it all, *I know deep down inside I am doing God's work*. I know that in my motherhood I am in an eternal partnership with Him. I am deeply moved that God finds His ultimate purpose and meaning in being a parent, even if some of His children make Him weep.[6]

The irony of a mom's situation is almost comical. The pressure on moms is greater than ever, and yet, we also receive less credit than ever for our work. It's not enough to raise well-adjusted children anymore. Now there are programs and guidelines and milestones and a million demands to meet—and then they start school. But when we understand that we aren't meant to answer to the world, but rather to the third childrearing "partner," our Father in Heaven, it can put motherhood into perspective.

Mother Knows Best

We are all unique in our methods. Each mother runs her family in a different way. So it makes sense that we would focus on the standards that we deem most important. It would be impossible to incorporate every single piece of expert advice out there. Not only do we not have the time or the sanity to do so, but many of those well-meaning books and articles contradict each other.

Ultimately, you and I are the experts in our families. We choose what to incorporate and what to discard. We keep our families focused on the right things as we struggle to make balanced meals. We try to keep up with schoolwork and teach our kids how to keep up a yard and clean the house. And it doesn't end until long after they step out into the world, hearts and stomachs full, ready and prepared to make a difference.

Do you love motherhood? Your answer is probably mixed. Yes, we all enjoy being moms, but man, is it hard! We are stretched to the limit, more maxed-out than a credit card, and weary in body and soul. Ours is the work of angels, but it *is* work.

> The pressure on moms is greater than ever, and yet, we also receive less credit than ever for our work.

Sometimes, on those particularly demanding days when I want to lock myself in my room, a little orphan face will come to my mind. She has short brown hair and dancing eyes, and the sound of her laugh sends thrills of joy through my body. The Romanian girl isn't my child. In fact, I will probably never see her again in this life. I couldn't do much to save her from a miserable situation, but that feeling she gave me of being needed and whole is now a part of my life every day. Watching my own children grow and learn as that little girl did gives me a deeper satisfaction than anything else could. Now I understand that I am making the world a better place.

We all are—one bedtime story and spilled cup at a time.

Notes:

1. Victor Hugo, *Ninety-Three* (New York: Carroll & Graf Publishers, 1988), 12.

2. William Ross Wallace, "What Rules the World," as quoted in *Errand of Angels: In Honor and Praise of Mothers* (American Fork, UT: Covenant Communications, 2007), 23.
3. Neal A. Maxwell, "The Women of God," *Ensign*, May 1978, 10.
4. George Washington, as quoted in *Errand of Angels: In Honor and Praise of Mothers* (American Fork, UT: Covenant Communications, 2007), 32.
5. Anonymous, as quoted by Jeffrey R. Holland, "Because She Is a Mother," *Ensign*, May 1997, 35.
6. Ibid.

2

How to Win When You Just Can't Win

"A mother is not a person to lean on, but a person to make leaning unnecessary."

—Dorothy Canfield Fisher [1]

WHAT TWO WORDS DESCRIBE YOUR LIFE AS A MOM?

For many of us, the first word is simple: "busy." What mother isn't busy? When someone asks us how we are doing, it is often the first word that jumps out. And if the other person is also a mother, she nods her head in complete understanding. Busyness is just part of the job description.

The second word, however, isn't one most would admit. A mom's life can get pretty crazy, but the busyness isn't even the hardest thing about raising kids. The hardest thing is often the guilt.

Why guilt? Here are some examples:

We feel guilty for cleaning instead of playing with the kids. We feel guilty for playing with the kids instead of cleaning.

We feel guilty for working instead of staying at home. We feel guilty for staying at home instead of working. (Yes, many of us really do have issues with this one!) We feel guilty for relaxing for a moment instead of playing with the kids (or scrubbing the bathtub, or running on the treadmill, or mowing a sick neighbor's lawn, or tearing the teenager away from his video game, or *finally* pulling those weeds).

In other words, we feel guilty. It's just what moms do.

The Supervisor

Most of us have spent at least some time in the workforce. We probably had managers or supervisors above us to help with training and motivation. They praised us when we did well and corrected us when we didn't.

Then we became mothers, and suddenly we were on our own. Now we don't answer to anyone else about our job (except for maybe society and, of course, Deity). There are no status meetings, no inspections. Moms have only one supervisor: ourselves. So we may make up for that by becoming our own worst critics. We correct and cross-check and second-guess ourselves until we can't see straight. Nothing we do is ever good enough for that persistent inner voice. We want our houses to be perfectly organized, sparkling clean, and impeccably decorated. We want our children to be adorable models of shining righteousness, complete with curled hair and ribbons. And when life gets in the way, which it inevitably does, we feel that we just aren't measuring up as mothers.

Elder Neal A. Maxwell counseled, "Some of us stand before no more harsh a judge than ourselves, a judge who stubbornly refuses to admit much happy evidence and who cares nothing for due process."[2]

Why the guilt? Why are we so hard on ourselves?

The Opposite of Guilt

Elder Russell M. Nelson said, "My heart goes out to conscientious saints, who, because of their shortcomings, allow feelings of depression to rob them of happiness in life. We all need to remember: men are that they might have joy—not guilt trips!"[3]

It's interesting that Elder Nelson phrases it that way, because it sounds as if he is implying that guilt and joy are opposites. If joy is a deep and residing contentment that comes from God, then what is guilt? In many cases, it comes only from ourselves—the offspring of unrealistic expectations and misguided intentions.

We expect perfection from ourselves and feel guilty when we fail. We look longingly behind us or around us. We see other moms and kick ourselves for being less organized in comparison. We watch our children fall short and throw that on the guilt pile too.

If joy is a deep and residing contentment that comes from God, then what is guilt? In many cases, it comes only from ourselves—the offspring of unrealistic expectations and misguided intentions.

It's no wonder that a woman who takes responsibility for everything—controllable or not—can't experience the joyful contentment of motherhood. It's no wonder that we sometimes want to throw in the towel.

The Impossible Game

My two older children are constantly in competition with each other. The six-year-old is very clever. She rigs their games so she always wins, which drives her four-year-old brother (and her mother) crazy. After a while, he realizes that he will never win. So he stops trying.

So many mothers have lives like that—a game that they can never win. The rules keep changing or seem stacked against them. Peace seems to taunt them from the distance, ever within sight but always just beyond their reach. Perhaps the "mom guilt" is keeping us from getting there. As Elder Nelson said, we cannot have peace and joy if we are racked with guilt.

President Dieter F. Uchtdorf said it beautifully in his talk to the women of the Church in 2011. He used as his metaphor the forget-me-not flower (he seems to understand women, doesn't he?) and counseled:

> God is fully aware that you and I are not perfect. Let me add: God is also fully aware that the people you think are perfect are not. And yet we spend so much time and energy comparing ourselves to others—usually comparing our weaknesses to their strengths. This drives us to create expectations for ourselves that are impossible to meet. As a result, we never celebrate our good efforts because they seem to be less than what someone else does.

In other words, many of us feel that our best efforts are never quite enough. We continually set the bar higher and higher, forgetting to look backward to rejoice in how far we've already come.

He continued:

> Everyone has strengths and weaknesses. It's wonderful that you have strengths. And it is part of your mortal experience that you do have weaknesses. . . . Keep working on it, but stop punishing yourself. Dear sisters, many of you are endlessly compassionate and patient with the weaknesses of others. Please remember also to be compassionate and patient with yourself.[4]

One of my favorite scripture passages is Mosiah 2:41, when King Benjamin explains the secret to finding peace and joy in this life and the next. He says, "I would desire that ye should consider on the blessed and happy state of those that keep the commandments of God. For behold, they are blessed in all things, both temporal and spiritual; and if they hold out faithful to the end they are received into heaven, that thereby they may dwell with God in a state of never-ending happiness."

Blessed. Happy. State of never-ending happiness. The ultimate fruits of peace and motherhood. The key is to recognize that yes, there is a difference between righteous initiative and beating ourselves up. The world does enough of that. Why do we help out by doing it to ourselves?

Beating the Guilt

The question is, how do we beat the guilt? How do we get out of the no-win game?

There's no easy answer. The game is different for every family. But the first solution may be to remember that there is only so much we can do as mothers. We need to learn to separate the things we can control from the things we can't. We'll talk about that in depth later.

Second, we need to remember that most of us are still learning about this whole parenting thing, and we make mistakes. As President Uchtdorf said, we aren't perfect. Often the only person expecting us to be perfect is ourselves.

A third solution may be allowing others to take responsibility for their own actions, including our own family members. That part can be hard. Perhaps you try to have meaningful scripture study and prayer every morning, but your teenager spreads himself on the floor and makes snoring sounds. Or perhaps you scrub during every spare moment with young children at your feet, cleaning and re-cleaning your apartment (and re-cleaning, and re-cleaning) only to have your well-meaning husband comment on the clutter in the living room. Let it slide. Hey, if our family members were perfect, they wouldn't still be down here with the rest of us!

It's tricky for a mom to avoid taking ownership of *everything.* I recently chucked the To-Do list and made it a Wish List instead—that way, if something actually did get done, hurray! Major bonus points for me.

Plus, I liked thinking about it that way. Many of my own expectations are wishes, really. It just took me a while to realize it. What was the worst thing that could happen if my kids were late to soccer practice? Would my children die of malnourishment if their lunch consisted of yet another PB&J sandwich instead of two servings of vegetables and protein? Would the world end if my four year-old wore his snow boots to play group in July? So everyone would know that we weren't perfect. Good. That would have been too exhausting an illusion to uphold, anyway. What a different world it would be if every family showed their (gasp!) imperfection.

It's okay to fall short sometimes. We don't become immortal the moment we give birth—we still have much to learn. But the chances are good that Heavenly Father is watching our progress with a Father's pride. As Elder David S. Baxter said, "If we have subjected ourselves to a constant barrage of self-criticism, let us recognize that we are better than we think we are!"[5]

The secret of the game is this: let's be the best mothers we can be, recognize the things we are doing right, and remember that we are works in progress. Let's laugh at our mistakes. Let's quit the internal whipping ceremonies and get on with our day. Only then will we find the inner peace that has been beckoning all along.

Notes

1. Dorothy Canfield Fisher, as quoted in *Errand of Angels: In Honor and Praise of Mothers* (American Fork, UT: Covenant Communications, 2007), 80.

2. Neal A. Maxwell, "Notwithstanding My Weakness," *Ensign*, November 1976, 13.
3. Russell M. Nelson, "Perfection Pending," *Ensign*, November 1995, 86.
4. Dieter F. Uchtdorf, "Forget Me Not," *Ensign*, November 2011, 120.
5. David S. Baxter, "Overcoming Feelings of Inadequacy," *Ensign*, August 2007, 11.

3

The Definition of Perfect

"There is no one perfect way to be a good mother."

—Elder M. Russell Ballard[1]

WHAT WAS YOUR FIRST THOUGHT WHEN YOU CAME UP OUT OF the waters of baptism? You let the air out of your lungs, rubbed your eyes, looked up at the grinning faces, and then—what?

I don't remember much about my baptism day, but I do remember that moment. My first thought was, "I'm clean!" followed by, "Now I'll just never sin and stay clean forever—perfect, just like Jesus was."

What a sweet tribute to an eight-year-old's reasoning. (It didn't work, by the way. I don't think I lasted five minutes.) In a way, though, the plan made sense. After all, the Savior *did* say, "Be ye therefore perfect, even as your Father which is in heaven is perfect" (Matthew 5:48).

Many Latter-day Saints consider this scripture to be the ultimate goal of every individual. So we read it, know it is true, and feel inspired to be perfect. We know that perfection is easily within our grasp and we can attain it by tweaking a couple minor things in our lives. Right?

Uh, no. Not exactly. Most of us read that scripture and think, "Hmm. Well, I'm just lucky to make it to sacrament meeting before the opening prayer," or, "Perfection? Ha. If my bathroom gets scrubbed more than once a month, I feel like Mother of the Year." Even on the best days, those have-it-all-together days, we still have to admit that perfection is painfully far away.

What is perfection? What did the Savior really mean when He asked us to become perfect? Our neighbors, our sisters at church, our fellow book club members, our coworkers, and even women of the world all have different ideas of what being the perfect woman entails.

Many of us take the scripture to mean that we should be perfect in everything we do, right *now*. We have a long list of expectations to be met before perfection can be reached, including a sparkling house or apartment that would pass any mother-in-law's white glove test, decked out in the latest interior design fashions and smelling of simmering vegetables fresh-picked from the garden. Our children turn in flawless homework that they were eager to complete. Our husbands arrive at the office in freshly starched collared shirts. We spend our days going down the checklist, doing everything we think we're supposed to do, when we're supposed to do it.

And eventually, the day comes when we read Matthew 5:48 and collapse in despair, saying, "There's no way! I just can't do it all!" And we are right. We can't. The Savior isn't asking us to, either.

What is perfection then, if not accomplishing everything under the sun that we are asked to do?

Perfection is Pending

Elder Russell M. Nelson explained his definition in his talk "Perfection Pending." Since Greek was the original language of the New Testament, he looked closely at the Greek word "perfect" as used in Matthew 5:48. It was derived from the Greek word *teleios*, which means "complete." He said:

> *Teleios* is an adjective derived from the noun *telos*, which means "end." The infinitive form of the verb is *teleiono*, which means "to reach a distant end, to be fully developed, to consummate, or to finish." Please note that the word does not imply "freedom from error"; it implies "achieving a distant objective." In fact, when writers of the Greek New Testament wished to describe perfection of behavior—precision or excellence of human effort—they did not employ a form of *teleios*; instead, they chose different words.[2]

Let's look at Matthew 5:48 again. "Be ye therefore perfect, even as your Father which is in heaven is perfect." Now let's substitute the Greek equivalent instead of the word "perfect," which changes it to "Be ye therefore *finished or complete*, even as your Father which is in heaven is *finished or complete*." This implies an end or change of state that doesn't just happen while we're here on earth cooking dinner.

This idea is confirmed in the Book of Mormon. The Savior was crucified, resurrected, and soon visited the Nephites in the New World. He repeated these words with a significant difference: "I would that ye should become perfect, *even as I*, or your Father who is in Heaven is perfect" (3 Nephi 12:48, emphasis added). Even the Savior of mankind, creator of worlds and the only being to pass through mortality spotlessly, was not truly perfect until *after* His resurrection.

Isn't that a great realization? We are not being commanded to be perfect right now. None of us can, at least not in this life. We are here on earth to find joy in life's lessons. If harsh expectations are constantly clamoring for attention in the back of our minds, maybe we can tell those expectations to go read Matthew 5:48 again.

Your Best Is Enough

Recently, at the grocery store, my three children were climbing all over the cart—literally—as I loaded the food at the checkout counter. It had been a long, irritating trip, and I was ready to collapse onto the dirty floor and wail with my toddler. I felt the eyes of the people behind us as I rushed to empty the cart and move it out of their way. Then I felt a hand on my shoulder.

It was an elderly woman. She held a simple basket with a few items, and I instantly felt guilty for not having allowed her to go ahead of me. But she smiled and said, "You are in the best time of your life, and you don't even know it."

Somehow her encouraging words made me feel that my best was good enough. My kids weren't perfect, and I certainly wasn't perfect, but it was all right.

Work in Progress

What is the definition of perfect? For me, the definition has changed since I was eight. Now it isn't about what I avoid or how much I accomplish or even how well I accomplish it, necessarily. It is about the person I am becoming.

Elder Oaks said:

> The Final Judgment is not just an evaluation of a sum total of good and evil acts—what we have *done*. It is an acknowledgment of the final effect of our acts and thoughts—what we have *become*. It is not enough for anyone just to go through the motions. The commandments, ordinances, and covenants of the gospel are not a list of deposits required to be made in some heavenly account. The gospel of Jesus Christ is a plan that shows us how to become what our Heavenly Father desires us to become.[3]

Now perfection isn't about what I avoid or how much I accomplish or even how well I accomplish it, necessarily. It is about the person I am becoming.

Even the best mothers have bad days, weeks, or even years. We fall short and make mistakes. We give in and give up and decide to try again. Isn't it comforting to know that we don't have to be perfect? That our best really is enough? That the Lord will accept our offering and make up the difference?

Bad days or good, all those thousands of offerings will eventually mold us into the mothers that we were always meant to be—and that is the *perfect* ending.

Notes

1. M. Russell Ballard, "Daughters of God," *Ensign*, May 2008, 108.
2. Russell M. Nelson, "Perfection Pending," *Ensign*, November 1995, 86.
3. Dallin H. Oaks, "The Challenge to Become," *Ensign*, November 2000, 32.

4

Spiritual Barnacles

"Motherhood has a very humanizing effect. Everything gets reduced to essentials."

—Meryl Streep [1]

I HATE SEAFOOD. IT'S NOT NECESSARILY THE TASTE—I CAN handle tuna sandwiches drowned in mayo and sweet pickles—but rather the smell. When my husband grills his latest fishing victim and that smell hits, I'm suddenly overcome with an urge to take his suits to the dry cleaners. Or buy more pantyhose. Or catch a sale at the scrapbooking store. He knows to air the house out really well, or I'll be out running errands for a long time.

Maybe we should have fish more often. He cooks, he cleans, he babysits, and I get a lot done. Sounds like a win-win to me.

I do, however, really like the ocean. It reminds me of my childhood in southern California. Perhaps that's why I'm so drawn to President Monson's story of the barnacles. Barnacles are shellfish that fasten themselves to a passing ship, stubbornly surrounding themselves with hard shells and refusing to detach. As more and more attach themselves to the ship, the drag slows the ship's progress. Eventually the captain has two choices: dock the ship and tear the barnacles away, or steer the ship to a freshwater environment that will kill them off.[2]

We all have barnacles in our lives—little energy-suckers that cause our own spiritual and emotional drag. Sometimes these barnacles attach in the form of unresolved sin or harsh words that we wish we could take back. Other times these barnacles come in the form of depression or other illness. Some of us simply have addictions or habits that drag us down.

Choose Your Destination

The first step of a journey is to decide where you want to end up. Why not start right now? Imagine your ideal life as a mother. What would you do, how would you act, and what would you say? How would your children treat you? How would your daily activities change?

If you're having trouble imagining such bliss, a good place to start is your patriarchal blessing. You'll find glimmers of divine potential throughout your own sacred piece of personal scripture. Your Father in Heaven has entrusted you with one of the greatest gifts any human being can receive, His precious child(ren). You have special gifts and talents that were intended to help you and your family as your ship bobs along life's waves. Read your blessing again and ask yourself these questions: Why was I given these gifts? What does Heavenly Father want me to do with them? What is my potential, and how can I get a little closer to that goal?

I feel the Spirit answering these questions constantly at church. The prevailing comfort of the Spirit allows me to reorient my life before another week abruptly begins. Other ways to receive inspiration about the potential of your family include daily doses of journal-writing, scripture study, and prayer. We'll talk more about these a bit later.

It's fine if these questions take a while to answer. Just remember: write it down in a journal or somewhere you can refer to it often. This goal will become your compass to help align your actions.

Seek and Destroy

The second step in the journey is to eliminate whatever is holding us back.

I grew up in a family where a perfect house was a major priority, if not *the* priority. Our house was decked out in flowers and lacy curtains like a little girl on Easter Sunday. Christmas alone was a week-long decorating ordeal. I grew to love designing a room from scratch with my mom, coordinating colors and matching patterns. I couldn't wait to have a house of my own someday.

So when my husband and I bought our first house as young parents, my first order of business was to impress our visitors with a stunning house. Each day, the moment the baby closed her eyes, I was in front of the TV watching my favorite decorating shows on HGTV and DIY Network. During the commercials I was online scouring websites for ideas. Even when the baby woke up, it was hard to tear myself away. My poor husband gave up and stopped watching TV with me in the evening. My passion had become an addiction.

When we moved into our second home a year later, finances were tighter and we decided not to subscribe to cable TV. What a significant decision that would become! Without the TV blaring every moment, the quiet that surrounded me was as sweet as candy. I was playing with my toddler on the precious day she started making her dolly "talk." I joined a play group, planted a garden, and took my little girl to the park almost every day. By the end of summer I had lost ten pounds. I looked great, had more energy, and finally felt that joyous fulfillment in motherhood that I had been craving.

It lifted my marriage too. When my husband came home from work, the Honey-Do list had shrunk (I'd say it disappeared, but let's face it—I didn't take the "How to Replace the Garbage Disposal" class). Instead of "Honey, we need to repaint our bedroom and install recessed lighting in the living room," it was "What would you like to do this Saturday, hon? Should we go to the lake?" Ahh. What a difference.

My barnacle? TV. A big, fat, stubborn barnacle.

The chances are excellent that we are already doing a great job in our homes. But if we still don't feel at peace, it may help to examine the problem closely. Barnacles can become apparent when we really ask ourselves the tough questions: "What is keeping me from feeling at peace? Does something in my life need to be tweaked a bit, or do I need a major overhaul?"

Perhaps there is the woman who wants to lose some baby weight—all four kids' worth—but there just isn't time to work out, and dieting only makes her frustrated and depressed. (Oh, honey. I understand.) Or maybe a neighbor wants to become debt-free so she can save for future college expenses. But of course, every time she saves a little money a tire blows out on the car or her son chips a tooth. Perhaps another mom wants to feel that warm, loving sensation of the Spirit again, but she feels so distant and alone that she doesn't know where to start—or constant contention keeps the Spirit far away. Maybe all of the above.

Barnacles can become apparent when we really ask ourselves the tough questions: "What is keeping me from feeling at peace? Does something in my life need to be tweaked a bit, or do I need a major overhaul?"

Those decorating shows did have one redeeming quality. When the makeover team descended upon an unsuspecting room, their first item of business was to remove everything from the room, staying or not. Then they brought back the critical pieces and left out everything else that didn't fit with their vision. The transformation was always incredible.

That approach may work for barnacles too. Let's look at the previous examples. The dieting sister may find that late-night aerobic DVDs relieve much of her stress, or cleaning out the pantry and removing the sources of temptation makes her diet more effective. The woman who struggled with debt elimination may discover that a stricter budget, or even getting the whole family involved with the goal, can carve out an extra $100 a month. Perhaps the mom who wants to curb contention cleans out the family's evening schedule and calendars family dinners, family home evening, and family prayer as first priority. That's a hard one, though, especially for families with teenagers. Some patterns are really hard to break.

Fresh Water

Sometimes we just have to start over—a clean slate, if you will. When there are thousands of barnacles attached to our boat, the simplest solution may not be to peel them off one at a time. Perhaps it's time to head for fresh water. Or in other words, we need to clear out the room entirely before we put back the pieces that belong.

President Ezra Taft Benson said, "When we put God first, all other things fall into their proper place or drop out of our lives."[3] It reminds me of a popular Relief Society lesson where sand, gravel, and rocks must fit into a jar. If you try to fit the sand and pebbles in first, the rocks don't fit. But if you put the rocks in first, everything else fills in around them, and *voila!,* everything fits. If only life were that easy, right?

It's one thing to arrange your life on paper. It's another thing altogether when the neighbor's son commits suicide or your mother is diagnosed with cancer. Life has a way of constantly making us change and rearrange our priorities. They say the one constant in life is change. Sometimes the only way to survive is in bite-sized chunks of daily inspiration.

Maybe that's why daily scripture study and prayer are two major "rocks" we are told to fit into the bottle—to invite the Spirit to help us as we make those constant decisions about diet, spending, and avoiding contention. Elder Richard G. Scott said that "We *become* what we want to *be* by consistently *being* what we want to *become* each day."[4]

Occasionally we will come across a barnacle that we can't get rid of on our own. These extra big, ultra-stubborn ones may need more than fresh water. They may need Living Water.

Living Water

I have a friend who had a very difficult childhood. Her father was abusive and she became depressed and resentful of the Church. Her appearance, her words, and her thoughts were angry and dark.

When I saw her again years later, the change was instantly apparent. She seemed lit up from the inside. She served faithfully in Church, served others eagerly, and listened to uplifting music. I was dumbfounded.

This dear friend had turned everything over to the Savior. He had given her a fresh start, and she was simply at peace. I almost envied her sense of joy and contentment with the world.

It can be incredibly difficult for some to give up the burdens we so diligently carry. We may tell ourselves we deserve our sins or struggles, or perhaps we don't dare give them up to someone else. But when the drag is so intense that our boat begins to sink, something must be done. That's where the Savior comes in. He can remove those burdens and send us lightly on our way to our eternal goals.

While traveling through Samaria, the Savior rested at Jacob's well. He asked a woman there for some water. Surprised, she asked why, as Jews usually avoided speaking to her people. After referring to what He called "living water," He told her, "Whosoever drinketh of this [well] water shall thirst again: But whosoever drinketh of the water that I shall give him shall never thirst; but the water that I shall give him shall be in him a well of water springing up into everlasting life" (John 4:9–14).

She probably thought it was a strange response. But then He went on to reveal His knowledge of her troubled past, including five husbands and a boyfriend. Surely she was touched by His loving demeanor and His invitation to partake of living water. Her history didn't matter, nor did her citizenship as a Samaritan.

> Life has a way of constantly making us change and rearrange our priorities.

The Savior's invitation is open to all of us, regardless of the type of barnacles we carry. Our ship may be large or small, dragging the ocean floor or just starting to slow. If there is something holding us back from where we would like to be, we can give our burdens away. We can pour out our hearts in prayer. We can speak with a bishop or branch president. We can become light upon the waves once again.

"Come unto me, all ye that labour and are heavy laden . . . for . . . my burden is light" (Matthew 11:28–30).

Drop those barnacles to the ocean floor, ladies. It's time to sail into the sunset.

Notes

1. Meryl Streep, as quoted by Bethenny Frankel, *A Place of Yes: 10 Rules for Getting Everything You Want Out of Life* (New York: Simon & Schuster, 2011), 292.
2. *Church News*, January 30, 1988, 16, as quoted by Thomas S. Monson, "Your Eternal Voyage," *Ensign*, May 2000, 46.
3. Ezra Taft Benson, "The Greatest Commandment—Love the Lord," *Ensign*, May 1988, 4.
4. Richard G. Scott, "The Transforming Power of Faith and Character," *Ensign*, November 2010, 43.

5

Choose the Best Food First

"We women have a lot to learn about simplifying our lives. We have to decide what is important and then move along at a pace that is comfortable for us. We have to develop the maturity to stop trying to prove something. We have to learn to be content with what we are."

—Marjorie Pay Hinckley[1]

THE FOOD AND DRUG ADMINISTRATION RECENTLY RETIRED the familiar "Food Pyramid" and replaced it with an icon of a plate. The plate is separated into four groups: grains, protein, fruits, and vegetables with a dairy "cup" above the plate.[2] It was intended to serve as a visual representation of how we should eat. Basically, America switched from a triangle full of food to a TV dinner package.

The idea, however, was that Americans should eat the right portions of the right foods to stay healthy—because unfortunately, many of us don't. Many American families—mine included—tend to call pizza and breadsticks a balanced meal.

Well, pizza has green peppers and tomatoes, right?

Taking Control of the Plate

Imagine that each day of your life is a plate. Think of your typical day in motherland. Do you have the right portions of the right activities? Are you balancing the important things with the just-for-fun things, or is the plate completely lopsided?

It is so easy to let the demands of the day lead well-intending mothers around. What mother doesn't feel a clutch of anxiety in the morning as she thinks of the demanding day ahead? We've all been there. So much of our day is planned for us—school, meals, laundry, housecleaning, sports, homework, callings, and perhaps even employment. No wonder we feel stressed and scattered! But we mothers have more power than we realize. We are the table servers who plan the "diet" of our family and ourselves—literally and figuratively.

There are so many amazing foods on life's buffet table, including juicy steak, savory chicken Alfredo pasta, and fine, we'll throw some lime-seared fish in there too (as long as I don't have to smell it). With all these filling and satisfying foods available, why are so many of us surviving on metaphorical pretzels and string cheese?

Much of the problem is a lack of planning. The vital things can get snuffed out by the less important things if we don't plan the important things first. There are probably a dozen bestselling business books that talk about priority lists and task-numbering. But interestingly, none of them are directly intended for the audience that uses time management techniques the most: mothers.

I have learned over the years that if I don't plan meals in advance before I go to the grocery store, we end up eating takeout a couple times a week. I get lazy and ask my husband to bring home a pizza (add breadsticks for a balanced meal), or we give in to the kids' demands and visit that colorful place with the play-place and chemical-laden food. We spend more money and eat worse, all because I failed to plan the week's meals in advance.

Planning. We really do have control over much of our plates. The key is to fill it with the best foods first—and then stop when we are full!

Decisions, Decisions

One thing we can all agree on is that the family comes first. After our husbands, the kids are the number-one priority. What mother wouldn't drop the phone and run to a toddler who has just injured himself? Or put off an appointment for ten minutes to listen sympathetically as a teenage daughter cries about something her friends said about her that day? Those decisions are more simple than others.

The hard part is priority number two. Sometimes even genuinely good things such as church callings, service, housecleaning, and being involved in the community can get in the way of priority number one. There are so many tantalizing options on the motherhood buffet these days. In fact, there are more opportunities today for women, particularly, than ever before. It's exciting, isn't it? Exciting and confusing at the same time. I love how Elder Neal A. Maxwell puts it:

> "So often our hardest choices are between competing and desirable alternatives. . . . Indeed, it is at the moral intersections—where time and talent and opportunities meet—that priorities, like traffic lights, are sorely needed. Quiet, sustained goodness is the order of heaven, not conspicuous but episodic busyness."[3]

Emma, my amazing sister-in-law and a single mother of two, is struggling to make ends meet while finishing her PhD. She told me that one Sunday night, while planning the coming week, there was not a single unscheduled hour. Every single minute of that week was taken by teaching, studying, dissertation work, her children's activities, and so on. Then her visiting teaching companion asked if Emma could make it to an appointment on Wednesday.

"I didn't have that hour. I didn't know how it would work," she said. "But somehow it did, and the week went better because of it. Now I make sure to plan the important things first—visiting teaching, family scriptures, family home evening, and church—because I know that everything important is in place. I'm not stressed. I really do feel at peace when I have my priorities right."

> There are so many tantalizing options on the motherhood buffet these days. In fact, there are more opportunities today for women, particularly, than ever before. It's exciting, isn't it? Exciting and confusing at the same time.

Like many other incredible mothers, Emma's goal for her family is eternal life, which means fulfilling her calling and teaching her kids the gospel are most important. Schooling wasn't a bad thing, just further down on the list. She filled her not-quite-large-enough plate with the best foods first, then allowed everything else to fill in around it. But it took a conscious decision on her part to slow down and *choose*.

The Self-Evaluation

Of course, in Emma's case, she was able to fit everything in. Often things don't fall into place quite that well. Making room for the important things usually means squeezing out some of those less-important activities, as painful as it is. But when we take control of the few things we can, life tends to align itself much more smoothly.

It may require a bit of self-evaluation. President Dieter F. Uchtdorf said:

> A wise man once distinguished between "the noble art of getting things done" and "a nobler art of leaving things undone." True "wisdom in life," he taught, consists of "the elimination of non-essentials." May I suggest that you periodically evaluate how you are doing in this area? What are the nonessential things that clutter your days and steal your time? What are the habits you may have developed that do not serve a useful purpose? What are the unfinished or unstarted things that could add vigor, meaning, and joy to your life?[4]

Choosing how to arrange the day will always be one of the hardest things about motherhood. It's a decision that we are constantly making and remaking as our families change.

In many ways, it is just like that iconic plate. Until they come up with a magic pill that replaces eating, we have to keep making the same "nutritious" decisions over and over. But the power to choose our own schedules and priorities, greater today than for any other generation, is a blessing. And who says that process has to be drudgery? Our Father in Heaven presents us with an entire buffet of savory options. Even if we can't enjoy everything at once, we have an entire lifetime to sample and enjoy new passions and activities.

Agency is such a blessing. So is the ability to feast upon the word of God as we choose what will best nourish ourselves and our children.

Feast? Now that's something we can all do. Bring on those mashed potatoes!

Notes

1. Marjorie Pay Hinckley, *Small and Simple Things* (Salt Lake City: Deseret Book, 2003) 148.
2. ChooseMyPlate.gov, created by U.S. Department of Agriculture.

3. Neal A. Maxwell, *Notwithstanding My Weakness* (Salt Lake City: Deseret Book, 1981) 5.
4. Dieter F. Uchtdorf, "As You Embark upon This New Era," in *Brigham Young University Speeches 2008–09* (Provo: Brigham Young University Press, 2009), 2; see also Lin Yutang, *The Importance of Living* (New York: William Morrow Paperbacks, 1937), 162, 10.

6

Jill-of-All-Trades

"God put me on earth to accomplish a certain number of things. Right now I'm so far behind, I will never die!"

—Anonymous [1]

I AM WOMAN. HEAR ME ROAR . . . OR SCREAM IN FRUSTRATION, rather, because I don't know when to quit, and I try to take on the whole world every day.

We all do it. Remember the admonition to avoid running faster than we have strength? Not only do many of us think we are the exception, but we consistently do so while carrying other people on our backs, talking on our cell phones, and planning our next Relief Society lesson. And when we finally collapse, we refuse to admit defeat and find ourselves looking around for alternative transportation instead. A bicycle maybe.

President Monson said, "The Apostle Paul likened life to a race. To the Hebrews he urged, 'Let us lay aside . . . the sin which doth so easily beset us, and let us run with patience the race that is set before us.' In our zeal, let us not overlook the sage counsel from Ecclesiastes: 'The race is not to the swift, nor the battle to the strong.' Actually, the prize belongs to him or her who endures to the end."[2]

Mothers are amazing. They universally exclaim, "Rest? Sit out the race? No way!" That kind of enthusiasm is wonderful. It allows us to brighten the lives of countless others and adds splashes of color to what can seem like drudgery.

But it is possible to be too focused on that finish line. In the daily race to get ahead and run even faster, we can forget about the things that matter most to us. It can be too easy to get caught up in the breakneck pace of competition. We can forget that the race isn't about speed but, as President Monson said, enduring to the end.

An inspiring wife and mother, Sister Patricia Holland, said:

> If I were Satan and wanted to destroy a society, I think I would stage a full-blown blitz on women. I would keep them so distraught and distracted that they would never find the calming strength and serenity for which their sex has always been known. Satan has effectively done that, catching us in the crunch of trying to be superhuman instead of striving to reach our unique, God-given potential within such diversity. He tauntingly teases us that if we don't have it all—fame, fortune, families, and fun, and have it all the time—we have been short-changed.[3]

The Roles of Women

Do you ever feel like the world is always dangling a carrot in your face? Me too. And just when you reach the carrot, someone snatches it away. We are ever chasing and never quite reaching that elusive having-it-all state, the place that surely will bring us peace.

We have messages from everywhere about our roles as women: movies, magazines, the prophets, our husbands, and even our children. (My six-year-old daughter once informed me that my job as mother was to do whatever she wanted. We had a nice long chat.) Some of these different expectations become so ingrained during childhood that life gets complicated when our own children come along. The messages seem varied and even contradictory. Ask friends and neighbors or even fellow sisters in the Church about their roles, and you'll get a dozen different opinions.

President Faust said, "You cannot do everything well at the same time. You cannot be a 100 percent wife, a 100 percent mother, a 100 percent church worker, a 100 percent career person, and a 100 percent public-service person at the same time."

Then he advised that although we couldn't do everything right now, in the words of Sarah Davidson, we could accomplish much of it "sequentially." Comparing the life of a mother to the song of a bird (sounds like a primary song, doesn't it?) he then said that a mother "does not need to try to sing all the verses of her song at the same time." [4]

Distractions

With three young children underfoot, I've learned a powerful parenting tool: distraction. When my kids are fighting over a toy truck, I find a race car that is equally enticing. When my toddler flails around like a trout on a hook while I change his diaper, I give him a book. Distraction even works on myself—running on the elliptical is so much less irritating while watching TV or reading. It's human nature. We are easily distracted.

The adversary knows this. He knows that a mother teaches by words and loving example. If he can distract us from our eternal perspective for long enough, he can create cracks in the core of the family. A little depression here, a bit of stress there. Sheri Dew said, "Satan baits us with perishable pleasures and preoccupations—our bank accounts, our wardrobes, even our waistlines—for he knows that where our treasure is, there will our hearts be also." [5]

Perhaps one of the great tests of this life is learning to focus and become proficient at one or two important things rather than being mediocre at a dozen.

This is one of my biggest weaknesses. I like to call it my Jill-of-All-Trades tendency. My mother calls it "being well-rounded." (I hope she refers to my personality and not my waistline.) Since childhood, I haven't stuck with one obsession long enough to finish anything. I was bored with baseball after a year, soccer after two, art after just one semester, and piano lessons after three years (although I did pick that one up again later). My horse obsession ended as soon as I got one. My children's scrapbooks are all half-done, my martial arts career ended at brown belt, and my house is *almost* organized. I have sold children's books from home and written for magazines and newspapers only when it sounded interesting.

> It's easy to do a lot of things somewhat well, throwing a bit of effort into each one. It's much harder to actually devote ourselves entirely to one or two very important things—especially such a thankless and frustrating job as motherhood.

And yet, through all my obsessions, my wonderful husband comes home from a hard day at work, sleeves rolled up, ready to support me in my latest quest, knowing well that it probably won't last past next week. He has it figured out. He is content with his role as husband and father. Everything else in his life is just extra credit, so to speak. He will have to pull me along in that great eternal race someday.

Shift from Quantity to Quality

Sister Patricia Holland quoted author Anne Morrow Lindbergh as saying that women today are "still searching. . . . With our pitchers [in hand] we attempt . . . to water a field, [instead of] a garden. We throw ourselves indiscriminately into the committees and causes. Not knowing how to feed the spirit, we try to muffle its demands in distractions."[6]

Isn't that great imagery? Instead of watering a garden, we're trying to water a field. When we feel too scattered to be at peace, maybe we're trying to spread ourselves too thin. We're giving 20 percent to too many things at once instead of 100 percent to the things that matter most.

Meanwhile, it could help to shift our focus from quantity to quality. It's easy to do a lot of things somewhat well, throwing a bit of effort into each one. It's much harder to actually devote ourselves entirely to one or two very important things—especially such a thankless and frustrating job as motherhood.

Mothers once cooked meals and did laundry as they chatted amicably with neighbors. Their homes were their world, and once the work was done, they could relax without guilt. Ironically, even with dishwashers and washing machines and vacuums and other time-saving devices, modern mothers are busier than ever.

Perhaps that's why driving is so irritating for me. It involves focusing on one simple task: driving. I have to resist the temptation to pick up trash between the seats or grab my cell phone and call someone. It takes real effort to resist filling every second with *something*. One of the challenges of modern-day motherhood—for me, anyway—isn't the busyness, but rather making the decision to sit still once in awhile.

In the words of President Kimball, let's return to "quiet, sane living."[7] Let's get a little more focused. Let's allow ourselves the pleasure of resting when we need it. Maybe a little peace is just what we modern mothers need to *feel* peace—to quench those frequent Jill-of-all-Trades tendencies.

Meanwhile, the race of life is still going on, and that's okay. Put the bicycle away and take a little water break. You may be surprised at how refreshed you feel.

Notes

1. Anonymous, as quoted by M. Russell Ballard, "Be an Example of the Believers," *Ensign*, November 1991.
2. Thomas S. Monson, "The Race of Life," *Ensign*, May 2012, 92.
3. Patricia Holland, "One Thing Needful: Becoming Women of Greater Faith in Christ," *Ensign*, October 1987, 29.
4. James E. Faust, "A Message to my Granddaughters: Becoming Great Women," *Ensign*, September 1986, 18–19.
5. Sheri L. Dew, "We are Women of God," *Ensign*, November 1999, 97.
6. Anne Morrow Lindbergh, *Gift from the Sea*, (New York: Pantheon Books, 1975) 45–46; as quoted by Patricia Holland, "One Thing Needful: Becoming Women of Greater Faith in Christ," *Ensign*, October 1987, 30.
7. Spencer W. Kimball, *Faith Precedes the Miracle* (Salt Lake City: Deseret Book, 1972), 265.

Puzzle Piece #2: Mother of Skill

A mother of skill realizes her unique power over the family environment. And yet, a skillful mom resists her inner control tendencies in favor of separating what she can control from what she can't—and finding peace in that decision.

7

The Power of Environment

"There is something within him which urges him to rise above himself, to control his environment, to master the body and all things physical and live in a higher and more beautiful world."

—President David O. McKay[1]

HAVE YOU EVER JUST FELT LIKE DRESSING UP? LIKE YOU JUST wanted to feel classy and beautiful—even though you knew that your morning would be spent organizing the pantry and scrubbing petrified honey drips off the shelves? When you feel pretty, you feel great about yourself, which makes you feel like a great mother, which results in a great day! All because you put on a little mascara and a cute blouse.

It's amazing the effect that the outside can have on the inside.

When you are feeling anything but peaceful, one thing you can change is the environment. If you sit at a drab cubicle all day, why not bring some photos and spruce it up with some fresh flowers? If you're like me and you spend much of your day in the kitchen (let's face it—I'm always preparing a meal or cleaning up after one), why not open the windows wide? Let in some light and fresh air? Play some happy music? Light a yummy candle?

There are dozens of little changes mothers can make to brighten their environment. Here are a few ideas:

- Happy or calm background music
- Brighter lighting
- Fresh air
- A favorite scent or candle
- Decorating update
- A deep cleaning session
- Favorite inspirational quotes hung conspicuously
- Organization
- Photos of loved ones, past and present
- Photos of the temple or the prophet

You'll notice that many of these are simply ideas to refresh the senses. Others require a little more work and planning (and a bigger block of time). Some, particularly those at the end, invite the Spirit. The Holy Ghost is probably the best and most important part of a peaceful family environment. It works both ways. When the Spirit is present, we feel comfortable and quieter on the inside; and when we feel at peace within, the Spirit can be present.

> The outside affects us all. The movies we allow our children to watch influence how they determine right and wrong. The music we listen to affects our emotions. Even the color of a wall can make us more relaxed or more energized.

Think about church for a moment. We dress in our Sunday best to show respect for the Lord's house, true, but we also do it for ourselves. We feel much more prepared to learn and worship when we have dressed ourselves appropriately than, say, if we wore jeans and sneakers. I know a family who wears their church clothing all day to remind themselves of the sacred nature of the Sabbath. It changes the way they think and act.

How about the temple? Every corner, every rug, every piece of glass in the chandeliers at the temple are painstakingly cleaned and cared for. It shows respect to our Heavenly Father and keeps it a sacred place, but it is also for us—because the environment affects the soul. We can feel the Spirit more strongly in a clean and beautiful place.

This concept applies everywhere. Businesses spend millions of dollars on the appearance of their buildings. Cities spend millions of dollars keeping their neighborhoods free of graffiti and garbage—because generally, the cleaner it is, the less likely there will be crime. The environment matters.

Now don't misunderstand. The point is not to induce a guilt trip about the current state of the kitchen. More importantly, we need to note the little things about our homes that affect those we live with, both positively and negatively. The connection between a person's emotional state and her environment is striking.

However, when a spotless house is impossible (isn't that usually the case?), perhaps getting the most important places up to par is sufficient. My mother was frequently ill while I was growing up. When I asked if she needed anything as she lay in bed, her frequent request was to clean her room for her. If I asked why, she would say that she couldn't heal in a messy room. The rest of the house was a disaster, of course, but as long as the most important room was clean, she was content.

The outside affects us all. The movies we allow our children to watch influence how they determine right and wrong. The music we listen to affects our emotions. Even the color of a wall can make us more relaxed or more energized.

Do you want to feel more peace? Try changing something in your environment. It may change so much more.

Note

1. David O. McKay, as quoted by Llewelyn R. McKay, *True to the Faith: From the Sermons and Discourses of David O. McKay* (Salt Lake City: Bookcraft, 1966), 244.

8

Judgment-Free Zone

"Home can be a heav'n on earth
When we are filled with love
Bringing happiness and joy
Rich blessings from above."[1]

MY HUSBAND GIVES FANTASTIC CHRISTMAS GIFTS. HIS secret? He asks what I want, and he goes out and gets it. Amazing, I know. One gift was particularly grand because he would have never gotten it for me if I hadn't asked—probably for fear of retaliation or mournful "You calling me fat?" allegations.

It was a gym membership.

Now let me explain. I have an odd relationship with gyms. My last membership involved walking into a wall of man sweat and jumping at the sound of metal weights dropping at either side. I learned to look straight ahead as I lifted, pushed, and pulled the rickety machines. If I happened to glance up, men with buzz cuts and tank tops would lick their lips and smirk as if to say, "Vutt a veakling. I eat veaklings for breakfast."

Well, I'm exaggerating a bit. I'm sure most of it was in my head. But feeling unfairly judged, I retreated to the comfort of my kick-boxing DVDs and ice cream, mourning the failure of my fitness goals.

But my husband's choice of gym was spot-on. One refreshing difference was clean equipment and good air circulation. However, the thing that impressed me most was their philosophy in large block letters on the wall: "You Belong!" To drive in the point, every single machine declared, "Judgment-Free Zone" and "No Critics Allowed."

One day, while working my flabby arms at the No Judgment Zone, I realized something. I felt completely at ease. The motto, displayed almost irritatingly often, was doing something vitally important. The patrons were friendly and courteous. Rather than looking down on those who struggled, they went out of their way to be supportive. The usual undercurrent of competition was replaced with a genuine desire to lift our fellow travelers on the road to fitness. The atmosphere was almost celestial.

Why wasn't my home more like that?

Suddenly I wanted to bring home that feeling of brotherhood. I wanted my own personal Judgment-Free Zone—a place where my daughter could come home excited to tell me about her day, rather than worried I'd flip out over a failed math test. A place where my husband could come home relieved rather than worried about getting attacked about the trash. I wanted us to be on the same team. I wanted my family to step inside the door, take a deep breath, and feel safe at last. Isn't that the whole point of a family? Isn't that what our homes are meant to become?

It may seem a bit unrealistic at times, especially when much of the family atmosphere depends on the rest of the family. We read about those seemingly perfect families or see them at church and wish our kids were more loving toward each other. Is it possible? If so, where on earth do we start?

If Mom Ain't Happy

Like any other change, a peaceful home has to begin with us. There's a saying that goes, "If Mom ain't happy, ain't nobody happy." Let's switch it around for a second: "If Mom's happy, everyone's happy." Maybe we mothers have more influence in our homes than we realize. The grumpy attitude of one family member spreads throughout the family like the chicken pox. Couldn't it work the other way around as well? Especially with the parent who (usually) sends everyone out the door with a lunch and a kiss?

Our own attitudes can have a remarkable influence on our family members. Imagine the confidence of a child who walks out that door feeling that she is unconditionally loved and important, or the positive effect of a son who truly believes the family motto, "You Belong!" Even our husbands can benefit from the unconditional acceptance of such an atmosphere.

Our own attitudes can have a remarkable influence on our family members.

When we feel contention in our homes, or a constant feeling of stress with certain family members, it may be helpful to implement a "Judgment Free" policy. This is not to say, of course, that family members can do whatever they want and get away with it. (If you have teenagers, you may have to remind them of this often.) What it means is that our homes are now havens of safety. We lift, encourage, and support the ones we love rather than tear down, criticize, and label them. We listen. We hold our tongues until we feel like our insides will explode. We try not to grimace as we say, "That must be hard. What are you going to do now?" instead of "What were you thinking?!"

It may take everyone a little time to adjust. If you have to hang your new motto on the wall in big bold letters, do it. Include it in your family rules or family mission statement or recite it every week at family home evening—whatever it takes. This change required a huge mental shift on my part, but it was interesting to see how the entire family followed my lead. It would have been more difficult had my children been older, of course. But it's never too late to start. The feeling in our home has been noticeably better since my gym epiphany.

We may not have attained "Super Mom" status yet, but maybe mothers have super powers after all. We can set a better tone for our families. Let's use our super powers to change our homes to Judgment-Free Zones. It could be the best change we ever make.

Notes

1. "Home Can Be a Heaven on Earth," *Hymns*, 298.

9

Control Baskets

"While we may not be able to control all that happens to us, we can control what happens inside us."

—Benjamin Franklin [1]

While my parents went through a divorce, my three younger sisters and I were blessed to meet with a well-known LDS counselor. He guided us through the rocky unknown and helped us stay close even though our family was falling apart. One piece of advice was particularly helpful: the Control Baskets.

He wisely recommended that we approach our difficulties by sorting them mentally into two baskets. (Being a "house of order" woman with an obsession with cute containers, I could totally relate to this analogy.) The first basket was labeled "Can Control" and the second "Can't Control."

"Then," he said, "you can throw the second basket in the mental lake, or imagine burning it, or whatever makes you feel better. But focus on what you can control, and forget about what you can't."

His message was profound. It changed my entire outlook on the divorce. As it became a part of my life, it affected even more—my parenting, my church calling, my financial concerns, and my relationship with my husband. Not only did it let me off the hook for things over which I had no control, but it reminded me about what was most important—my husband, my kids, and my role as a daughter of God.

Control Issues

Many of us consider ourselves "control freaks." (I am the President of Control Freaks Anonymous. Nice to meet you.) Such tendencies aren't necessarily bad. Control Freak moms often have many traits to be admired, including initiative and focus. We get things done when most other people would give up. We are content with no less than our best, and we prefer to have each messy string in our lives tied up neatly. But sometimes such tendencies can be counterproductive. Somewhere in the process of grasping wildly for control, we end up giving it away instead.

Have you ever heard yourself say, "When such-and-such happens, then I can be happy," or, "If only so-and-so had done this, then everything would be fine." Sometimes we hinge our entire emotional state on things over which we have little control. In a way, we are giving away our own agency and hanging it on someone else's decisions or actions.

I know a woman who has always struggled with her weight. She eats healthy food and exercises, and has even tried medical treatments, but to no avail. At first glance, that's all people see about her. But once they get to know her, they forget about her appearance because her soul radiates from within so brightly. This woman always has a smile. She seems to pulse with positive energy, causing a warm glow in the hearts of those with whom she interacts. They walk away feeling that they are the most important people around. This woman has effectively focused on what she can control, and she is dearly loved for it.

Mike Schlappi, a graduate of my Utah high school, was a popular student and athlete. A sudden shooting accident left him paralyzed just weeks before his fifteenth birthday. Rather than brooding about it, he took up wheelchair basketball. He eventually represented the United States at the Paralympics and became a world champion. He focused on what he could control.[2]

> We are content with no less than our best, and we prefer to have each messy string in our lives tied up neatly. But sometimes such tendencies can be counterproductive. Somewhere in the process of grasping wildly for control, we end up giving it away instead.

Think about the following scenarios. Which should be in the "Can Control" basket and which should be in the "Can't Control" basket?

- Your husband's pay is cut at work in efforts to avoid layoffs. You meet to discuss the family budget.
- Your preschooler dumps gravel down the kitchen sink. When you run the disposal later, it breaks.
- Your visiting teaching ladies aren't available for you to come by during the last week of the month.
- Your yard is becoming overrun by weeds, but your job keeps you too busy to do yard work.
- Your teenage daughter is frustrated because prom is a week away and she hasn't been asked.
- Your oldest son decides not to serve a mission.
- You don't have enough money to pay your college student's tuition next semester.
- The car breaks down, so you have to walk your young children to school. They are frequently late.

These are tough ones, because many have elements of both. Sometimes things happen that we could have prevented or affected in some way. The hardest part of the Control Basket process is to stop the mental floggings and move on. Even if we may not have handled things very well in the past, we can still do it right from here on out. "Where do we go from here?" can eventually replace the "Why didn't I"s and "If only"s of life. Sorting these events into Can/Can't Control baskets helps us focus our attention on the future rather than the past. Only then can we truly feel at peace.

Control as a Trial

Mothers are intuitively sensitive and self-sacrificing beings. We want the best for our children. We feel frustrated when things don't go as planned or when our children are struggling. It can be so painful to watch someone we love go through a difficult trial. Any mom would take a child's heavy burden upon herself in a heartbeat if she could. But watching others struggle with trials and with their own agency can also be one of the greatest trials we ourselves endure. Sometimes we can't take the burden away. It goes in the "Can't Control" basket. But we can often make it easier to bear. We toss that realization into the "Can Control" bin.

We need to take responsibility for ourselves and our own actions, and somehow move on from there. Life can be crippling in its intensity sometimes, but it shouldn't overcome us for long. The poet Walt Whitman said, "O while I live to be the ruler of life, not a slave, / To meet life as a powerful conqueror, / . . . And nothing exterior shall ever take command of me."[3]

It takes maturity to realize that we can't control everything, especially for us "control freaks." We can't control our children. We know that they are not "blank slates" as philosopher John Locke believed, but rather come with personalities, preferences, and the light of Christ. They come with the powerful capacity to change the world rather than be defined by it.

Just as we can't control our children, we can't control our spouses. We can't control our brothers or sisters or parents (*especially* our parents). Ultimately, I can only control myself. Maybe that's a good thing. I don't want to be held responsible for things other people do, anyway. I'm having a hard enough time with myself!

Take control and responsibility of what you can, throw away the rest, and take a deep, cleansing breath. Doesn't that feel great? Congratulations. You've taken a major step toward peaceful motherhood.

Note

1. Benjamin Franklin, as quoted by Willard Stawski, *That Ye May Prosper: Meaningful Lessons from the Book of Mormon* (Springville, UT: Cedar Fort, 2007), 106.
2. Mike Schlappi, *Shot Happens* (Draper, UT: Schlappi Communications/Brigham Distributing, 2009), 8, 101–119.
3. Walt Whitman, as quoted by Shira Wolosky, *Walt Whitman: Poetry & Prose* (Michigan: The Toby Press, 2003), "A Song of Joys," Book XI, *Leaves of Grass*, 206.

Puzzle Piece #3

Mother of Work

A mother of work keeps a house of order, but she also understands that relationships are more important than her tasks. She thinks of her work as an opportunity to serve, grow, and teach rather than drudgery. She knows that keeping a balance between work and play is essential to keeping her enthusiasm for motherhood. Such a mother confronts her inhibitions and enjoys life with her family.

10

House of Order

"The privilege to work is a gift, the power to work is a blessing, the love of work is success."

—Elder David O. McKay [1]

FOR SEVERAL DAYS AFTER WE MOVED, I STARED AT THE STRANGE new flower beds in utter dismay. We'd come from a townhome community where I hadn't had to do any yard maintenance. I couldn't even keep a houseplant alive, much less care for a yard full of landscaping. If gardeners truly have "green thumbs," my thumbs would have been considered fluorescent orange or something.

My mother-in-law, however, had a perpetually beautiful flower garden. It seemed to sprout up spontaneously in early spring and bloom effortlessly all summer. One day, frustrated that my best efforts weren't making our own front walk resemble anything but a weed garden, I asked how she did it.

Her secret: Wherever there's nothing, that's where weeds will grow.

It took a few more summers of failed gardening attempts to realize how profound her statement was. The ground's default, so to speak, is weeds. They can grow almost anywhere—heavy shade, hot sun, tiny cracks, scarce water, and everywhere in between. But it takes a purposeful and concerted effort to make flowers grow.

Flowers require consistency. They need fresh air, sunshine, and nutrient-rich soil. Flowers take work. It's worth it, though. Once established, flowers will eventually crowd out weeds.

It can be much the same when we are faced with running a household. The default of a home is chaos. It takes determination, clutter removal, and "planting" new organizational habits to create order. It also takes commitment and a whole lot of elbow grease. Just like a garden, it is a constant work in progress. We are never truly done.

But it does get better with time. Even the sturdiest flowers need a few years to fully develop their root system. It takes a while, but after a million reminders and years of practice, our kids will start to pick it up (pardon the pun). Keeping a clean house shouldn't simply be a mom's job. It should be the entire family's way of life—and it starts with our expectations.

House of Order

Messes tend to affect me emotionally. I'll see a trail of dirty clothes leading from the back door to the recently cleaned bathroom, which of course is now covered in sand and mud, and my heart beats a little faster with irritation. As I grab the cleaning supply tote, I'll recall a Relief Society lesson about our homes being similar to temples and feel that familiar frustration in my gut. Later I'll scan a messy room in disappointment and catch a glimpse of the famous organization scripture on my wall, Doctrine and Covenants 88:119—"Organize yourselves; prepare every needful thing; and establish a house, even a house of prayer, a house of fasting, a house of faith, a house of learning, a house of glory, a house of order, a house of God."

You may read that and give a sigh of relief, thinking how similar that is to your own home (if so, please email me your secret). Or, if you're like the rest of us, you'll feel a twinge of panic. You may be overwhelmed by its expectations. At first the verse seems to incorporate several very different concepts. After all, what do fasting and prayer have to do with order?

> It does get better with time. Even the sturdiest flowers need a few years to fully develop their root system.

But in a way it also makes sense. When we have a house of order, we *can* have a house of God. When our homes are (at least somewhat) organized, we can have the Spirit with us.

Sister Julie Beck explained this concept well. She said:

> I started thinking about my home and family and what was necessary to create an environment or climate where the Spirit of the Lord would be. There were some necessary things to take care of. Homemaking took on a new meaning for me. I wanted to make a home where the Spirit of the Lord was present. That meant that even mundane tasks, like picking things up and cleaning, became necessary to keep a house of order. I wanted to model my house after the temple. Though that is the ideal, it has never been that perfect. We have to live there after all. A house is peopled with people. People make messes, and we can't be little soldiers, but it made a difference to me to know that I wanted a house of order. It became a priority to make a place where the Spirit of the Lord could come.[2]

Sister Beck's goals are remarkably similar to the list in the Doctrine and Covenants. She admitted that her home could never be perfect (good news for us—even a former General Relief Society president's home isn't impeccably clean all the time), but clarified that she wanted her home to be "a place where the Spirit of the Lord could come."

Now let's assume we all want a clean house. Perhaps it's not a question of motivation at this point. Perhaps the real question is *how*?

Get the Family Involved

The Little Red Hen story was obviously written by someone who understood kids. The mother hen decides to make some bread for her family. She asks who will help her plant the wheat, but everyone bails. So she does it herself. Then she asks who will help her harvest the wheat, and everyone disappears again. She fruitlessly begs for help with taking the wheat to the mill (surely a difficult task for a little chicken), grinding the wheat, and baking the bread. Finally the bread is made, and suddenly her family shows up again to partake of the fruit of her labor. But since she did all the work, the little red hen eats the bread by herself. This little mom had remarkable vision and perseverance. Especially for a chicken.

Sometimes organization is a lonely task. Our children don't really care. Even our spouses may consider it beyond their job description (my husband would use the words "chick project"). But the fact is, this work is for the family, and it should be implemented by the family. Otherwise it will never stick.

Children who organize their own toys will be more likely to put them away. Spouses who help put away their own laundry may be more careful to hang up their clean clothing (I know, that's a stretch). Kids who have to clean up after themselves are less likely to make a mess. Moms are homemakers, it is true, but we aren't slaves. We are guiding our families in the right direction. (However, if we find ourselves barking like a drill sergeant—or a "little soldier," as Julie Beck called it—something has gone wrong.) This is a group effort. It is absolutely vital that we involve our families in the process.

Break It Down

One of the overwhelming things about our new yard was that

each flower bed—and there were several—was packed with weeds and wild grass. My husband and I would have to pull out everything before we could think about planting. It felt like an impossible task. We could see our Saturdays quickly dwindling into oblivion.

To make the project more manageable, we broke up the project into zones. We attacked the flower beds by the driveway first, since those were seen from the street. Slowly the weeds came out, the fertilizer was gently tilled in, and the colorful new flowers found a home. (Our children "helped," of course.) The instant lift in our yard was astounding. My husband and I grinned at each other and thought, *Maybe we can do this after all!*

Again, organization is similar. A house of order can seem utterly unreachable, especially when there is ten times more stuff than there are people. It may help to go through the same steps we did.

- First, break the project up into small, more manageable zones.
- Second, decide where you would like to start. I like to begin in a high-impact area first.
- Third, take everything out and scrub it clean (this is a good time to involve family members). Imagine you are a home designer and remove everything before you decide what really needs to go back. You may be surprised how little needs to stay. When you put objects back, be sure to save space for the future.
- And fourth, admire your work! Show it to your family, point out where everything goes, and enjoy that feeling of satisfaction. So what if the rest of the house seems to have exploded while you attacked your closet? At least that closet looks fantastic. Each little baby step forward is still a step in the right direction.

Don't Give Up

It's true that motherhood often involves swimming against a relentless current of clutter and junk. That's just part of having a family. But when we take it one project at a time, our efforts begin to add up.

It's a slow process. I usually limit myself to one organizing project a week. It's realistic, but the pace can be frustrating at times. The important thing is that I'm trying, my home is becoming more organized every week, and my family is practicing new habits that will make our home more peaceful.

> Each little baby step forward is still a step in the right direction.

Just keep in mind that those weeds will keep coming. Once the flowers are planted, we still have to maintain them, which can be the hardest part of all. In especially busy periods of time, the garden may fill up with weeds again. But the flowers will eventually grow in thick and full, and the new habits will finally be firmly established. And the most important part is that we will have taught our children the value of a "house of order," a peaceful haven. Our homes will be places where our family members can grow accustomed to feeling the peaceful presence of the Holy Ghost.

Hopefully by then my flower beds will look just like my mother-in-law's garden.

Well, a girl can dream, anyway.

Notes

1. David O. McKay, as quoted by Kristi Linton, "Money Matter$" *The New Era*, September 2004.
2. Julie B. Beck, "Choose Ye This Day to Serve the Lord," BYU Women's Conference, April 29, 2010.

11

The Purpose of the Task

"Women who know are nurturers. . . . Nurturing requires organization, patience, love, and work."

—Sister Julie B. Beck [1]

THE BEST THING ABOUT ENTERING COLLEGE WAS FINALLY BEING able to learn what I *wanted* to learn. After years of being told which classes to take and regurgitating facts, I could finally take classes that sounded interesting. One such class was called "Work and Relationships in the Home."

After the first day, I knew exactly what the premise was: "The purpose of the task is to strengthen the relationship."[2] In fact, that sentence was drilled into us so well that ten years later, it still affects me. Think about it. Everyone, especially mothers, is here for a specific reason. It may be just a guess, but I don't think that reason is robotic floor-sweeping and dish-washing. Those mundane tasks need to be done, of course. But they aren't the real purpose.

In fact, the class taught that even having a clean floor isn't the real purpose of cleaning a floor. The real purpose is people. We do it for the ones we love—not just because it keeps the toddler from putting week-old macaroni into his mouth, or even because it teaches a teenage daughter to have a high standard of cleanliness. It's because work, both for and with our children, can strengthen relationships. We grow closer to those with whom we work. Period.

Take math homework, for example. I have a friend who, as a child, really struggled with math. She just couldn't get it. Her math-major father decided to conquer the problem and began to sit with her each night as she did homework. His goal was to help her understand so her grade could improve. To him, that was the purpose of the task. But for her, each session ended in tears of frustration. She felt that he didn't understand her. She thought that he wouldn't love her unless she, as he believed, fixed her lack of understanding with a flip of a switch in her brain. What could have been a valuable father-daughter experience became a dreaded nightly argument.

The "purpose" approach would have been for that father to remember that his relationship with his daughter was ultimately the most important thing. An understanding of math was necessary, true, but it was secondary. A child's foundation as a valuable member of an eternal family, and a belief that no failed math test could possibly change her value, was really the number one goal. The purpose of math homework was to strengthen the relationship.

The purpose of 2:00 a.m. feedings? To strengthen the relationship. The purpose of making dinner? To strengthen the relationship. The purpose of laundry? Budgeting? Spring cleaning? Food storage inventory? Endless Band-Aid applications? It applies to anything. Once you get the concept, it changes your entire outlook on motherhood. It changes those mundane, everyday chores into precious moments.

Harmon Killebrew, a baseball player, once told a story of his purpose-driven father. The two brothers spent much of their time playing sports in the yard with their dad. Their mother would come out and say, "You're tearing up the grass." "We're not raising grass here," he would reply. "We're raising boys."[3]

Sure, it's hard to let my daughter do the vacuuming when I can do it faster and better. It drives me crazy when the kids get ingredients all over the kitchen when they "cook." And I can't help when my son's attempts at sweeping a floor resemble hockey more than housecleaning. But when I remember that the relationship is more important than the task, I become more patient with the wobbly carpet lines, the crusty food in the corners, and the powdery white flour sprinkled on the counter tops. And best of all, my kids actually enjoy helping Mom. For as long as that lasts, I'm going to ignore the perfectionist within and enjoy their adorable efforts.

Try it. Make today or tomorrow your "purpose" day, and see how it changes your life—one task at a time.

Notes

1. Julie B. Beck, "Mothers Who Know," *Ensign*, October 2007.
2. A. Lynn Scoresby, PhD, retired BYU professor.
3. Harmon Killebrew, as quoted in by Pamela J. Bailey, *Sanctuary: Creating a Blessed Place to Live and Love* (West Bloomfield: Warner Books, 2006) 50.

12

How to Not Make Everything Work

"Learn to like your work. Learn to say 'This is my work, my glory, not my doom.'"

—President David O. McKay [1]

WITH A TO-DO LIST LONGER THAN A ROLL OF FLOSS, WE OFTEN ask, "How do I make everything work?" Perhaps the right question is actually, "How can I make everything *not* work?"

Work. A dreaded word—almost as dreaded as the other four-letter word: *diet.* Of course they're both necessary concepts, and we sludge our way through them when forced to do so. But when they are over, we feel like we can finally get back to our lives. What we don't realize is that only decades ago, work *was* life.

Elder Maxwell once stood in general conference and displayed almost one hundred ribbons. He had won them for his prize pigs during his childhood. He said that raising pigs to compete at the fair had been hard, but it had taught him how to work.

"Most young men my age did similar work," he continued. "Back then . . . we were all poor together, and we didn't know it. Work was a given. Today, for some, receiving is a given."[2]

One of the hardest jobs of a modern mother is curbing entitlement and teaching our children responsibility. And the best way to accomplish both is through work. But how do we do that when we don't even like work ourselves?

Weeks after my wedding, a friend asked how married life was going. She had been married for several years already. I told her delightedly how much I enjoyed cooking for my new husband and cleaning our two-bedroom apartment. She chuckled and said, "Yeah, that won't last long. Just wait." At first I brushed off her pessimism. But eight years and three children later, the novelty of running a household has definitely gotten old. If I had a piece of chocolate for every time I swept the floor under the high chair each day, I'd be fifteen pounds heavier.

Finding Joy in Work

Some of my favorite mothers have one thing in common. Each woman has the ability to find joy in her life's work. Whether they work full-time or stay at home, these women "whistle while they work," figuratively and literally. They truly understand how to not make everything into work.

A good question to ask ourselves is, "What is my attitude toward work?" Chances are, our own attitudes are probably reflected by those of our children. (A horrid thought, isn't it?)

I love Fridays. Not only do they kick off a weekend, but Friday is also the day I finish my deep cleaning. By Friday evening the laundry is freshly washed, folded, and put neatly away. The wood floors gleam, the vacuumed carpet is soft and clean (despite the kid-created wobbly lines), and my husband and I can turn to the weekend with a light step and little stress. The only way to describe that feeling of accomplishment, in my opinion, is simple joy.

This joy can be found in the small tasks. I love the light in my daughter's expression when she gets positive recognition for a school project we worked on together. Those evenings when my freshly bathed and sleepy kids snuggle with me as we read stories are priceless. Pure joy. The grassy smell of a freshly mown lawn is addicting to me—it represents summer in its truest form. And the raised eyebrow from my food-critic husband when he likes his dinner makes me smile. He is still surprised when my cooking turns out well. Apparently it doesn't happen very often. That's okay—I enjoy that part too.

Teaching Kids to Work

So how do we pass that on to our children? How can we stop making everything work? Bishop Burton said that "Even young children can begin to experience the benefits of working when they are involved in household chores and in service to others. Wise parents will work alongside their children, will provide frequent praise, and will make sure no task is overwhelming."[3]

Mary Poppins was wiser than many of us, singing, "A spoonful of sugar makes the medicine go down" as she cleaned with the children.[4] My husband discovered one day that this musical method really does work. He blasts each child's favorite song, and they clean as fast as they can while the song plays, then stop abruptly when the song ends.

My kids also have job charts that they have to complete if they want allowance the following Saturday. If they grumble or ignore a request to clean up, they have two choices: take an extra chore from a cup or be my "slave" for five minutes. We all enjoy the slave game because they have to do everything I say, whether it is washing doorknobs or doing silly cartwheels. It's the spoonful of sugar that makes work *not* work.

I've heard of families who separate into teams and make cleaning a competition. Others may assign each child a "zone" to keep clean. My own mother paid us in fake money and then provided a store once a week where we could spend it on candy and small toys.

There are a thousand ways to do it, and our methods are constantly changing with our families. But the important thing is that work is a part of life, it's part of being a family, and it's helping our kids become well-adjusted people. It isn't only our grandparents who understand the value of a job well done. President Monson said that "When you learn to work while you're young, the habit stays with you."[5] Not only will that habit stay with our kids, but it will teach them gratitude and responsibility as well.

Work Ethic

Elder F. David Stanley said, "The frightening disappearance of work as a part of our basic ethic is alarming." While that rings true for many of us, his next words are even more stunning. He continues, "We constantly hear the statements, 'It's too hard,' 'Give me something easier,' 'I want it now,' 'I can't wait that long' coming from our young people. The ugly disease of 'nothing to do' is growing in epidemic proportions among us."[6]

Elder Stanley is right on, at least in my household. My kids have less work than I did as a child and twice as many toys. And yet, the more they receive, the more they want. (I'm sure this characteristic isn't unique only to children. I find myself acting the same way all too often.)

There's a reason the world calls ungrateful, irresponsible children "spoiled." Once such kids think the world exists to make them happy, it's almost impossible to change that belief. Work is a much harder lesson to learn as a nineteen year-old missionary than as an eager toddler.

With this in mind, I try to be careful how I describe the work of parenthood in front of my kids. Raising them is a joyful job, not drudgery, and I want my kids to know it. I hope they understand that everything else that demands my time is a side note to my true calling as their mother. Being a mom is usually very fulfilling. As Alma said, "Why should I desire more than to perform the work to which I have been called?" (Alma 29:6).

When we work together as well as apart, and focus on not making everything work, our children will be better prepared to face the realities of adulthood—and we'll all be happier as well.

Notes

1. David O. McKay, as quoted by Llewelyn R. McKay, *Stepping Stones to an Abundant Life* (Salt Lake City: Deseret Book, 1971), 116.
2. Neal A. Maxwell, "Put Your Shoulder to the Wheel," *Ensign*, May 1998, 37.
3. H. David Burton, "The Blessing of Work," *Ensign*, December 2009, 44.
4. *Mary Poppins*, Walt Disney Studios, 1964. Directed by Robert Stevenson, produced by Walt Disney.
5. Thomas S. Monson, "Friend to Friend," *Friend*, October 1981, 7.
6. F. David Stanley, "The Principle of Work," *Ensign*, May 1993, 44.

13

Balance

Daniel: When do I learn how to punch?
Miyagi: Better learn balance. Balance is key. Balance good, karate good. Balance bad, better pack up, go home. Understand?

—*The Karate Kid* [1]

In college, I discovered kung fu. It quickly became an addiction—in part, I must admit, because I was dating a black belt. But mastering a new set of skills during a fun workout gave me great satisfaction.

A core concept in kung fu is, as you've probably guessed, balance. If you're off-balance, you can't block the attack of your adversary, much less counterattack. An unbalanced martial artist doesn't last long during a sparring match.

But balance isn't just for the Karate Kid. Balance is even more important for women who are raising families. Elder Ballard counseled, "remember [that] too much of anything in life can throw us off-balance. At the same time, too little of the important things can do the same thing."[2]

We are told that our days should be filled with productivity. No problem there! A mom works hard all day and is on-call at night. The hard part is actually putting down the glass cleaner and getting on the floor to play with our children. We feel that if we aren't filling every second, we are wasting precious time.

Learn Your Limits

Robert Millet, in his book *Life in Christ,* gave a rather poignant description of the modern Latter-day Saint. He spoke of members in general, but the description probably fits women better than anyone. First he warned that a person relying too much upon her own abilities blocks herself in her progress and weighs herself down with guilt.

Then, referring to us generally, he said that people "seek to redouble their effort—to work harder. If the present pace does not eradicate the problem, they decide to run faster. Too often what follows is a type of spiritual diminishing returns—exhaustion and additional frustration. The answer to all problems is not necessarily more and harder work, particularly in regard to spiritual matters. The answer is often to learn our limits and do what we can, then turn to the Lord for assistance."[3]

First, we should learn our limits. Second, we should use the Control Baskets method (see chapter 9). And third, we should take a break from the race once in awhile, as mentioned in an earlier chapter. But simply resting usually isn't enough. Play, in the form of hobbies or even board games with the kids, can rejuvenate our minds and refuel the mommy reserves within.

We know that rest and play are an important combination for mothers. We can work ourselves crazy, but without a break, we lose our enthusiasm for motherhood. Look at the Family Proclamation. It's no mistake that the principles of "work and wholesome recreational activities" are listed together.[4]

Work and play. They're the "yin" and "yang" of family time, so to speak.

So where is the line, then?

Brigham Young once gave an interesting guideline to time management. He said, "Life is best enjoyed when time periods are evenly divided between labor, sleep and recreation . . . all people should spend one-third of their time in recreation . . . never idleness."[5]

Brother Brigham's "eight hour labor, eight hour sleep, eight hour play" recommendation, while often considered too simplistic for our day, may still have merit. A typical mom's day tends to be much more lopsided: six hours of sleep, sixteen hours of work, and two hours of exhausted zoning out in front of the TV, for example. Of course the situation is different for every woman. And it is interesting that he uses the word "idleness." Perhaps one of the keys to finding that ever-elusive balance is defining the difference between three seemingly similar opposites of work: play, rest, and idleness.

The Opposites of Work

Play can be many things to many different people. Some people think running ten miles in the crisp morning air is play. I consider that cruel and unusual punishment. But I also consider researching and writing a challenging paper to be play, while most people avoid it like a hot stove. Art, photography, dance, car detailing, or flying airplanes—we all have passions that make us come alive. I know a woman who feels the most at peace wielding power tools amid furniture plans and the smell of sawdust. Even building a block tower with a toddler or a enjoying family soccer competition in the backyard can be very invigorating for a mother's soul. Such passions can constitute a mother's version of play.

Idleness, a word rarely used anymore, is very different from play. It is defined as "avoiding work," "lacking substance," and "to move lazily and without purpose."[6] This is a tricky one. Some activities that are very useful can also be considered idleness.

One such activity for me is browsing the Internet. I tell myself I'm keeping in touch with friends (which is occasionally true) or "resting" (which is rarely true), when in reality I'm just avoiding a sink full of dishes. This can be a sticky topic for some people, because the Internet can do a lot of good too. Social networking has been shown to ease the painful loneliness of stay-at-home moms and single mothers, and many of us enjoy a network of support through blogging. But I will say that when I began to write this book, I traded browsing my favorite websites for writing time. It was shocking how much quality time suddenly opened up in my schedule. I now understand why the Lord says not to "idle away thy time, neither shalt thou bury thy talent that it may not be known" (Doctrine and Covenants 60:13).

> Art, photography, dance, car detailing, or flying airplanes—we all have passions that make us come alive. Such passions can constitute a mother's version of play.

The third word, *rest*, is foreign to many mothers. Rest is defined as "peace," "quiet relaxation," and "relief or freedom from disquiet."[7] Often the only time we experience this is when the kids are asleep at night, and maybe not even then. But there is something satisfying about the late-night whooshing of the dishwasher and folding that last load of laundry. We need those times of reflection to refill the spiritual reserves within. The more active and crazy the day, the more vital it is to have downtime. Kids need it, husbands need it, and moms *especially* need it. Rest makes us more patient, more appreciative, and more in tune with the Spirit. It really is about balance.

Once we understand how to find a balance between work and its opposites—play, idleness, and rest—we can focus on the most rejuvenating activities. This helps us to avoid squandering the precious time we have here in mortality. Our lives are simply a dot on the line of eternity, and the time during which we are raising our children is even shorter. Busyness isn't necessarily productiveness.

Housewife and Mother

It's okay to put some tasks on the shelf so we can play with our children. The clutter on the living room floor will not spontaneously combust if it stays there another day (although that would be nice). The house won't be quarantined for a messy refrigerator. Our kids come first.

A favorite poem, called "Excuse This House," says:

> Some houses try to hide the fact
> that children shelter there.
> Ours boasts of it quite openly,
> the signs are everywhere.
> For smears are on the windows,
> little smudges on the door.
> I should apologize I guess,
> for toys strewn on the floor.
> But I sat down with the children
> and we laughed and played and read.
> And if the doorbell doesn't shine
> their eyes will shine instead.
> For when at times I'm forced to choose
> the one job or the other,
> I want to be a housewife
> but first I'll be a Mother! [8]

That's balance—recognizing what is most important. We do it all the time. We hire babysitters and go on dates with our dashing husbands. We go to the temple to regroup and rejuvenate our spirits. We even allow ourselves to eat dessert sometimes. (Didn't Marie Antoinette say, "Let them eat cake?"[9] I wholeheartedly agree.)

Sue Woodman said, "Living by basic good-mothering guidelines enables a mom to blend the responsibilities of parenthood with its joys; to know when to stand her ground and when to be flexible; and to absorb the lessons of the parenting gurus while also trusting her inner voice when it reasons that another cookie isn't worth fighting over, or that her child won't suffer irreparable trauma if, once in a while, Mom puts her own needs first."[10]

The better we take care of our needs, the better we can handle the needs of our family members. Work and play; yin and yang.

Find a balance, Daniel-san.

Notes

1. *The Karate Kid*, 1984. Directed by John G. Avildsen, written by Robert Mark Kamen.
2. M. Russell Ballard, "Keeping Life's Demands in Balance," *Ensign*, May 1987, 16.
3. Robert Millet, *Life in Christ* (Salt Lake City: Bookcraft, 1990) 47–48.
4. The First Presidency, "The Family: A Proclamation to the World," paragraph 7, published by The Church of Jesus Christ of Latter-day Saints. Read by Gordon B. Hinckley in General Relief Society meeting, September 23, 1995.
5. Brigham Young, quoted by Susa Young Gates and Leah D. Widtsoe, *The Life Story of Brigham Young* (The MacMillan Company, 1930), 251.
6. *The American Heritage College Dictionary*, Fourth Edition (Boston: Houghton Mifflin Company, 2004), 688.

7. Ibid., 1185.
8. Author unknown.
9. Often attributed to Marie Antoinette, although there is some debate on the subject.
10. Sue Woodman, as quoted in *Errand of Angels*, 60.

14

Mommies at Play

"The only way to get through life is to laugh your way through it. You either have to laugh or cry. I prefer to laugh. Crying gives me a headache."

—Marjorie Pay Hinckley [1]

Recently, I visited a dear friend in California. As she busied herself in the kitchen, her seven-year-old son came in from the backyard, looking for someone to play with. Since I was the only one available, he stood squarely in front of me, held up his stick-and-twine bow and arrow, and formally announced, "I would like to hold a shooting contest. Whoever shoots their arrow the furthest wins. Do you accept the challenge?"

Well, who could say no to that?

The funny thing is, I think he even beat me. I need to practice my archery skills.

I love the stories about the Prophet Joseph Smith, who was often seen playing games with the children outside. Some people thought it was improper for a prophet to be doing such things. But maybe he understood something that others didn't.

It can be hard for moms to let loose and play sometimes. Why is that? We were all children once. Inevitably, though, at some point we can forget how to play. It seems that many of us become serious and responsible just before our kids come along, and then we have to re-learn how to have fun. We stuff our heads so full of checklists and priority-setting that we shove away thoughts of non-accomplishment because we are being good, efficient mothers. It takes raising kids to realize that we have to find a balance.

While we teach our children to integrate work into their play, they teach us to integrate play into our work. And sometimes the line between the two can become pretty fuzzy. Those are the best moments, aren't they? Children and parents working and playing together, building a foundation that will last their entire lives.

It's not about the list of things we have to do or want to do, but rather about the people we are serving. All we do every day is for our children in the long run, isn't it? So why not drop the broom and have a tickle fight for a few minutes?

My kids love the "kissing monster" game. They sit on my lap and I say in my most intimidating voice, "What does the kissing monster eat?" They tentatively say, "Kisses!" and I "attack" them with kisses. Even my one-year-old loves it. I think my children feel more loved when Mommy is silly than when we have a clean house. Good thing, because ours is nothing like a clean house.

Can you think of a family that is just plain silly? A family that lives life out loud and with gusto? The Price family is the first to come to my mind. On the surface they seem like a typical family. They have three children from college to elementary school. But you don't have to look far to see that they are far from typical.

The father, Dale, was in a motorcycle accident years back and lost his leg. Rather than brooding, he started a paintball company. The name? "Pegleg Paintball." That gives you a sense of this family's quirky humor.

My children call their home the "Halloween House." From September through November, their front yard becomes a mysterious graveyard—complete with headstones, caskets, the reaper, and a hearse or two. On Halloween night the yard becomes a smoky, howling attraction for families from all over the county.

That's not all. On a recent fall morning at the start of the school year, Dale followed his teenage son outside and waved as the bus drove away. Later his embarrassed son asked him to never do it again. Many fathers would have done as his son had asked, but not Dale. The next morning he was outside, blatantly waving at the bus in a Chargers football uniform.

That was the beginning of the "waving at the bus" campaign. Every day for an entire school year Dale wore a different costume to wave his son goodbye. Nothing was off limits. His costumes ranged from a hula girl (with the coconut bra, of course) to Nacho Libre. One day he was "John," sitting comfortably on an actual toilet, newspaper in hand. Soon the family was being covered by local news, then national news, then international news. The strange costumed man with the peg leg became a celebrity. And what's more, his son knew without a doubt that he was loved.

> While we teach our children to integrate work into their play, they teach us to integrate play into our work.

It's okay to be silly sometimes. Why sit quietly at a stoplight when you can turn up the music and rock out with your kids? Why sit on a bench at the park when you can chase them around, pretending to be a shark? Why grumble about how often your son plays the Wii when you can challenge him to a game? Kids love when we jump in and have fun with them.

It's a little unfair that dads have a reputation for being the fun parents, while mothers are considered the disciplinarians and the slave drivers. Why not switch it up a little? When we make the effort to play, it only makes the "serious mom stuff" that much more effective. A popular quote says that "People don't care how much you know until they know how much you care."[2] All the discipline in the world won't make your child feel truly loved unless you throw in a spoonful of sugar.

Childhood is so fleeting. We trudge through the muddy years of raising our children, thinking they'll never end, then suddenly they're gone. Author Anna Quindlen said, "The biggest mistake I made [as a parent] is the one that most of us make: . . . I did not live in the moment enough. . . . I wish I had treasured the *doing* a little more and the *getting it done* a little less."[3]

Let's enjoy those precious moments—and our kids—just a little more. And don't forget to brush up on those archery skills. You never know when they'll come in handy.

Notes

1. Marjorie Pay Hinckley, as quoted by Virginia H. Pearce, *Glimpses Into the Life and Heart of Marjorie Pay Hinckley* (Salt Lake City: Deseret Book, 1999), 107.
2. John C. Maxwell, *The 21 Irrefutable Laws of Leadership: Follow Them and People Will Follow You* (Nashville: Maxwell Motivation, 1998), 60.
3. Anna Quindlen, *Loud and Clear* (New York: Random House, 2004), 10–11.

Puzzle Piece #4

Mother of Faith

A mother of faith knows she is on the Lord's side. She realizes her divine potential and refuses to allow trials to shake her faith for long. She sees her little children as examples of innocence and charity. She also knows that her children have their agency and may choose a different course than the one she would prefer. A faithful mom understands that she will never be alone in raising her family. She realizes that one of the best ways to refill the pitcher is to turn to the Lord in prayer and scripture study. She is determined to be an example of integrity. And she knows that she is not Superwoman, but she can still be an incredible mother as she follows the direction of the Spirit.

15

The Game Is Set

"The future of this world has long been declared; the final outcome between good and evil is already known. There is absolutely no question as to who wins because the victory has already been posted on the scoreboard. The only really strange thing in all of this is that we are still down here on the field trying to decide which team's jersey we want to wear!"

—Elder Jeffrey R. Holland [1]

In the third year of our marriage, my husband began to complain that his hand felt tingly. It felt as if he had slept on it wrong, but the feeling didn't subside. After a few days, we became more concerned as it became difficult for him to type on the keyboard at work and even play his beloved guitar. Soon the numbness crept up his arm and spread throughout his left side.

Alarmed, we left our toddler with her grandparents and rushed to the emergency room. It was there that we first heard those dreaded words: Multiple Sclerosis.

MS had always been disconcerting to me. I knew it as a condition that had caused many of my husband's clients at the law firm to declare themselves "disabled" and apply for Social Security. I also knew that it often robbed the use of limbs and that people with

MS often ended up in wheelchairs. Suddenly our future—children, grandchildren, a mission or two—seemed very unclear. Would I now become the financial supporter? Would he ever play the guitar again? Could a cure possibly be found in the coming years?

But the most prevailing thought was, *Why?*

Rules of the Game

Why do bad things happen? We all know the answer when tough things happen to others. Our hearts break for our friends and neighbors when tragedy strikes. But not until it's our turn do we understand the true life-consuming, foundation-shaking nature of trials. Somehow the quick answers "Because life is a test" or "It must be God's will" don't quite answer the question. Our soul craves a knowledge that the Supreme Being of the universe has not abandoned us, that the painful changes in our lives have a purpose.

Orson F. Whitney said that "no pain that we suffer, no trial we experience is wasted," because it helps us develop patience, fortitude, and humility, and it purifies our hearts, making us more tender and charitable and more like our Father and Mother in heaven.[2]

Elder Neal A. Maxwell knew this well. He fought a painful eight-year battle with leukemia. He said:

> How can you and I really expect to glide naively through life, as if to say, "Lord, give me experience, but not grief, not sorrow, not pain, not opposition, not betrayal, and certainly not to be forsaken. Keep from me, Lord, all those experiences which made Thee what Thou art! Then, let me come and dwell with Thee and fully share Thy joy!"[3]

There really is a fundamental change that occurs when something upheaves our lives. We suddenly feel the pain of others more acutely. We know how to better serve those who suffer. While well-meaning friends mistakenly tell grieving parents potentially painful things like, "Don't worry, the Lord needed him more than you did," or "At least you have two other children," we can put an arm around them and say, "I am so sorry. I love you so much." While others thoughtlessly judge, criticize, dismiss, or condemn, we look for every opportunity to build and support. Our own pain helps us to ease the pain of others.

We Choose Our Team

While racked with emotion and desperately trying to sort through the pieces of our lives, we really only have two options: faith or fear. It may seem simplistic or even dramatic, but it is true. They cannot exist together. They are opposing teams, if you will. The moment fear creeps in, faith flees. The Savior broke the rules of physics to allow his Apostle Peter to walk on water. He wouldn't, however, break the laws of agency. Once Peter's faith wavered, His sustaining power waned. He can only help as far as our faith will let Him.

> Our soul craves a knowledge that the Supreme Being of the universe has not abandoned us, that the painful changes in our lives have a purpose.

When these life-changing moments hit, we may want to run away rather than face the problem head-on. Often this desire is understandable. A friend of mine received a devastating blow when her husband left her and their six children. Her first reaction was to give up. The thought of getting dressed, making meals, facing her children, and fighting the world alone was just too overwhelming. What she really wanted to do was just give in—to succumb to the pain. But she didn't. This amazing woman faced her trial squarely in the face every day as she struggled to keep her family together. She chose to have faith and press on. Eventually she remarried and her children are now grown.

Imagine if she had cursed God, left the Church, and spent her life bitterly reliving the past. Her children's testimonies (and subsequently her grandchildren's church activity) could have been severely affected. Not to mention that she would have traded the source of true comfort for a source of anger and depression. But luckily, she chose the winning team instead. (That sounds like a breakfast cereal slogan, doesn't it?) That was perhaps the most crucial decision she would ever make.

The Team Captain

During times of trial, it may seem that the Team Captain has taken a water break. But we know from the scriptures that we are not abandoned.

In many ways, another analogy—that of life being an exam—has merit. Students taking a test may have to come up with their own answers, but the Teacher is always nearby. And in most cases, I think the ultimate Teacher even cheats a little. Not only is it an "open book" exam, but He sends His "aide" to whisper helpful hints in the ears of those who will listen.

We also know that our Team Captain suffers with us as well as for us. Moses 7:28–32 shows that the Lord mourns over those who are lost: "They are the workmanship of mine own hands . . . and gave I unto man his agency . . . that they should love one another, that they should choose me, their Father; but behold, they are without affection, and they hate their own blood."

And the grandest part of all is that our Team Captain isn't a has-been who cares little whether His team wins or loses. The Savior, knowing that His friend Lazarus would soon return to his mortal body, still wept with Mary (John 11:35). He suffers with us. Christ has already won the game singlehandedly. He is fully invested—His entire existence has been dedicated to you and me. Of course He will not abandon us in our time of desperate need.

Imagine if the Lord had raised Moses to a life of wealth and nobility, groomed him for leadership, officiated miracles such as the river turning to blood and the untold numbers of eldest children's deaths (very symbolic, as we know), and finally won the freedom of a vast multitude of people who escaped the most degrading of circumstances—only to abandon Moses at the Red Sea.

Imagine if He had chosen Lehi, shown him visions and called him to be a prophet, warned him about a threat to his life, guided his family to safety, answered his son Nephi's fervent prayers for a testimony, and guided the brothers to retrieve the plates of brass that would affect the salvation of hundreds of thousands of future descendents—only to leave Nephi to the whims of Laban.

Our lives may not have oceans parting before us or dramatic visions, but each of us has been guided, protected, and cherished by a loving Father throughout our lives. We all have different family situations. We all have different trials. We all have strengths and weaknesses, special gifts and personal struggles. Yet, looking back, it is humbling to see how carefully our lives have been shaped by an all-knowing hand.

Cling to that knowledge when the hard times come. If they haven't yet, they surely will. It's the game plan. But we can take comfort that we are on the winning team.

My husband's symptoms only lasted a couple months before the numbness faded away. Other sufferers aren't so lucky, and we feel extremely blessed. It has been five years since his symptoms disappeared. Someday they will likely return. But until then, we will appreciate each symptom-free day more fully than we ever could have before.

When the opposition mounts and the clock presses on, let's choose the side of faith. Only then can we truly be at peace.

Notes

1. Jeffrey R. Holland in email correspondence, as quoted by John Bytheway, *When Times are Tough* (Salt Lake City: Deseret Book, 2010), 30–31.
2. Orson F. Whitney, as quoted by Spencer W. Kimball, *Faith Precedes the Miracle*, 98.
3. Neal A. Maxwell, "Lest Ye Be Wearied and Faint in Your Minds," *Ensign*, May 1991, 88.

16

The Seeds of Divine Potential

"We cannot change our past . . . we cannot change the fact that people will act in a certain way. We also cannot change the inevitable. The only thing we can do is play on the one string we have, and that is our attitude. I am convinced that life is 10 percent what happens to me and 90 percent how I react to it."

—Charles Swindoll, Christian author[1]

LAST FALL, A NEARBY STRIP MALL COVERED AN OUTDOOR flowerbed with sod. I suppose the maintenance had become too inconvenient. The sod grew in nicely over the winter and looked nearly flawless—that is, until spring. Suddenly yellow and red shoots were coming up through the grass. They were bulbs planted in previous years that were fulfilling the measure of their creation, grass or no grass. The landscapers had completely forgotten about the seeds waiting quietly beneath the cold ground.

We also have the seeds of divine potential within us. We are literal spirit children of an actual, living God. It's not a fluffy, warm-fuzzy concept. It's truth. We are programmed with the potential to become like our Father. And being the perfect Gardener that He is,

He has already provided us with everything we need. The world can pile on as many barriers as it wants. But if we stay focused, eventually we will reach our potential as daughters of God.

Pat, a mother in my neighborhood, is a powerful example of a flower growing through the grass. At first glance, Pat is a single working mother raising a teenage girl. She is active in the Church and has a strong testimony. The clincher: Pat has cerebral palsy.

Her story began from a complicated birth. The hospital nurse predicted that Pat would never talk, walk, or go to school. The newborn couldn't even suck a bottle, so her mother poured formula into her mouth from a shot glass.

With physical and speech therapy, she was able to defy the nurse's grim prediction. She started walking with difficulty by age three. Soon little Pat could even say a few words. But the braces on her legs and the constant scabs on her knees and elbows from falling down made her self-conscious. She became determined to live a regular life.

By third grade she joined her peers at a "normal" elementary school. She somehow managed to keep up with her classmates even though it was difficult to make herself understood. She was given extra time on tests and was excused from physical education classes, but those were the only allowances young Pat would accept. In seventh grade she began helping the librarian while her classmates went to PE class. That experience sparked an interest and a knack for cataloging that would change her future.

Pat worked so hard that she was admitted to BYU, but the daily hike to campus from the dorm proved to be a forty-five-minute ordeal. Rather than giving up, she found a bicycle that would work and pressed on.

Obtaining her bachelor's degree did little to satisfy her hunger. She entered graduate school, earned her master's degree, and has now worked for years at the BYU library. Despite her difficulty in communicating and walking, her coworkers have admired that same determined spark in Pat that has lifted the lives of so many others.

Pat had finally fulfilled her dream of leading a nearly "normal" life—except in one area. At age forty-one, Pat's desire to be a mother became the last and most important dream of all. She began the adoption process. A two-year-old girl from India soon joined her, and suddenly they were a family. It was a small family, and an unusual one at that. But they were complete.

"There are lots of things that I can't do," Pat once told me. "But the things that I can do, I will do." And she has.

> The world can pile on as many barriers as it wants. But if we stay focused, eventually we will reach our potential as daughters of God.

There are so many amazing women struggling their way through each day. These women refuse to give up. The very thought of their potential shriveling up and dying in the cold soil is not an option for them. They will push through no matter what life piles on top of them. These are the "noble and great ones" saved for the last days (Abraham 3:22–23). And guess what? You are one of them!

President Dieter F. Uchtdorf said:

> Sisters, wherever you are, whatever your circumstances may be, you are not forgotten. No matter how dark your days may seem, no matter how insignificant you may feel, no matter how overshadowed you think you may be, your Heavenly Father has not forgotten you. In fact, He loves you with an infinite love. . . . He who created and knows the stars knows you and your name—you are the daughters of His kingdom. [2]

You may not feel like a daughter in His kingdom when your house is constantly a train wreck and your kids often look like they just rolled out of bed when they go to school. So what if you let Elmo babysit your toddler occasionally and your gourmet dinner menu is Hamburger Helper and canned pears? Maybe your teenager goes on dates in an old '89 clunker and your kids are wearing fourth-generation cleats to soccer practice. The thing that matters is that you're still trying. You're "playing on the one string you have," as Swindoll so eloquently put it.

It's a noble gesture to press on for yourself. But people who refuse to give up are also examples to those around them. As Pat says, "If everyone had a perfect body, what would we learn? We wouldn't have opportunities to learn love, compassion, charity, sympathy, patience, and understanding. He gives us trials for our own growth, but also for the growth and learning of others."

Let's cling to our potential. When we allow the rich soil of trials to nourish us instead of bury us, eventually we will enjoy the bright sunlight reserved for the strongest of souls.

Notes

1. Charles Swindoll, as quoted by John C. Maxwell, *Developing the Leader Within You* (Nashville: Nelson Business, 1993), 98.
2. Dieter F. Uchtdorf, "Forget Me Not," *Ensign*, November 2011, 122–123.

17

Childish or Childlike?

"When I grow up, I want to be a little boy."

—Joseph Heller, author[1]

I LOVE THE STORIES OF CHRIST. THE PARABLES ARE SO MEANINGful, the beatitudes are pure truth, and the four gospels feel like the lifeblood of our religion. But there has always been one puzzling scripture for me. In Matthew 18:2–3, the Savior commanded us to "become as little children." Does that strike you as a bit strange?

Don't get me wrong. Children are adorable, mine especially (I'm sure yours are cute too). But why become *like* them? Kids argue. They yell, they talk back, and they definitely don't enjoy sharing or taking turns. Kids bang around and run over things and pull each other's hair. If we should become like children, does that mean I can start dumping my food on the floor at dinner? That I can leave my messes for others to clean up? That doesn't sound too bad, actually.

This interesting concept isn't mentioned in passing, either. Children are recognized as examples several times across the scriptures. Isaiah prophesied that "A little child shall lead [us]" (Isaiah 11:6). We see it again in Mosiah 3:19: "For the natural man is an enemy to God . . . and will be, forever and ever, unless he . . . becometh as a child."

Children and Christ

My favorite chapter of the Book of Mormon, 3 Nephi 17, reveals that Jesus Christ visited the ancient Americans after His death. He had very limited time there. What did He do? He blessed the children one by one and prayed for them (verse 21).

Why did he bless the children? Why not bless their parents? After the traumatic experience of natural disasters and likely losing loved ones or even their homes, the adults probably needed a blessing much more. And we know that those children were destined to lead a life of joy in the gospel (4 Nephi 1:14–16). So why bless the children?

What is the connection between a child and the Savior that is so profound?

Children and Faith

Perhaps it is the Christlike faith of children that draws the Savior to them. Mostly untried and full of unquestioning hope, they still retain much of their innocence. Children can be mischievous, of course, and they learn through self-discovery, which usually results in a giant mess. Each child comes complete with a personality and a sense of wonder and adventure. But the brightness of hope inherent in a little child seems to bring with it a remembrance of something eternally familiar.

I don't know of anything sweeter than my toddler's wet kisses and delighted giggles. He hasn't learned much about the dangers of the outside world, but he knows the most important things: his family loves him, his home is a safe and fascinating place, and his needs will always be met. He has an unwavering trust in his caregivers. I hope we can live up to that trust.

I also learn about Christlike purity from my preschooler, who understands more about charity than many adults. He is so self-sacrificing, so affectionate, and so willing to give that I feel humbled just to be his mother. His preschool teacher recently pulled me aside as the school year ended, her face full of emotion as she admitted that my son's bright smile and "Hi teacher!" greeting every morning made her feel that her day was now complete—even though it had just begun.

There is something so carefree about childhood. There certainly is something to be said for childlike innocence.

It feels as if I'm breaking the news of Santa Claus when I talk to my children about stranger danger. I watch their little countenances grow concerned and see their innocence slip away thread by thread. It is the scary darkness of the world around us that tears it away from them. I see the process with each passing month as they go to school, dance class, and karate and play with friends: a word here, a story there. The bubble of protection is slowly being eroded away.

This is a natural process. Somehow I don't think that the scriptures are asking us to stay innocent. In fact, that is contrary to God's plan, isn't it? We came here to learn as much as possible about life and the people around us. Perhaps the key is that, once we "grow up," we need to somehow incorporate a childlike faith and confidence in God while keeping a wary eye on the world.

Adults and Childlike Faith

Some people just have it figured out. President Gordon B. Hinckley was one of those people. He likely knew more about the evils and the dark corners of the world than most of us, yet he was one of the most unfailingly optimistic people who ever lived.

My mother-in-law is another example. Her entire life is dedicated to two things: her family and service. When she isn't serving her children or her husband, she is out serving someone else in need. One day, while listening to me grumble about someone I was struggling to forgive, this amazing woman told me, "Just remember, don't treat people the way they are now. Treat them how they can eventually become, and they're more likely to become it." Knowing the difficult situations of some of her family members, that outlook was even more amazing. Such an attitude of ultimate confidence in the human soul is something to be admired.

Are these people naive? I don't think so. In fact, both have had such devastating trials in their lives that they could easily have written off the world as a painful place. I think they just choose to hope despite the odds. They choose to see the best in people. They have powerful faith in God's will. It reminds me of Mosiah's words again: "[Become] as a child, submissive, meek, humble, patient, full of love, willing to submit to all things which the Lord seeth fit to inflict upon him, even as a child doth submit to his father" (Mosiah 3:19).

Humble. Patient. Loving. Submissive. These words sound a lot like a Christlike person. In fact, they sound just like Christ Himself. And He is the ultimate example of a child submitting to His Father. In an emotionally poignant scripture we learn that, at the peak of the Savior's incomprehensible pain, He begged, "Father, take this cup from me. Nevertheless not what I will, but what thou wilt" (Mark 14:38). So when we are commanded to become as a child, aren't we really being asked to become more like Him?

He is the ultimate example of a child submitting to His Father. So when we are com manded to become as a child, aren't we really being asked to become more like Him?

President Eyring said:

> We may well see being like a child as being weak. . . . But King Benajmin, who understood as well as any mortal what it meant to be a man of strength and courage, makes it clear

> that to be like a child is not to be childish. It is to be like the Savior, who prayed to His Father for strength to be able to do His will and then did it. Our natures must be changed to become as a child to gain the strength we must have to be safe in the times of moral peril.[2]

It is indeed a beautiful concept. That childlike pureness of heart, that complete and utter acceptance of whatever Heavenly Father desires, is perhaps the closest we can get to being one in purpose with God. It is at those times that we learn the most about ourselves. It is also at those times that we realize how powerful a blessing motherhood truly is.

I feel honored to have such delightful examples of Christlike faith right here in my own home. While I am teaching them to be adults, I know they are teaching me to become more like a child. Hopefully someday we will both succeed.

Notes

1. Joseph Heller, *Something Happened* (New York: Random House, 1974), 340.
2. Henry B. Eyring, "As A Child," *Ensign*, May 2006, http://www.lds.org/ensign/2006/05/as-a-child?lang=eng.

18

Counting Blessings

"You could have an experience with the gift of the Holy Ghost today. You could begin a private prayer with thanks. You could start to count your blessings, and then pause for a moment. If you exercise faith, and with the gift of the Holy Ghost, you will find that memories of other blessings will flood into your mind. If you begin to express gratitude for each of them, your prayer may take a little longer than usual. Remembrance will come. And so will gratitude."

—President Henry B. Eyring[1]

One of my favorite classic movies of all time is "White Christmas." It's our traditional holiday present-wrapping entertainment. It has a song in which Bob and Betty meet in the kitchen on a sleepless night. They discuss their inability to fall asleep because of too much on their minds. Then they break into song:

When I'm worried and I can't sleep
I count my blessings instead of sheep
And I fall asleep
Counting my blessings

> When my bankroll is getting small
> I think of when I had none at all
> And I fall asleep
> Counting my blessings.[2]

There's a remarkable effect that occurs during hard times. When our problems are all we can see, the Lord reminds us through multiple sources that we need to widen our focus. He asks us to see the good in our lives as well as the difficult parts.

Irving Berlin's advice about counting our blessings is not new to us today, nor was it new in 1954 when he wrote it. The famous hymn "Count Your Blessings" advises a similar approach:

> When upon life's billows you are tempest-tossed,
> When you are discouraged, thinking all is lost,
> Count your many blessings; name them one by one,
> And it will surprise you what the Lord has done.[3]

We see the same message scattered throughout the scriptures.

- Old Testament: "O Lord my God, I will give thanks unto thee forever" (Psalm 30:12).
- New Testament: "In every thing give thanks: for this is the will of God" (Thessalonians 5:18).
- Book of Mormon: "And when thou risest in the morning let thy heart be full of thanks unto God" (Alma 37:37).

I even find myself repeatedly teaching it to my children:

- "Say thank you."
- "'Ew, gross' isn't what we say at dinner—how about 'thank you' instead?"
- "You get what you get, and you don't throw a fit."

I wonder how many times Heavenly Father has wanted to say these things to His own spirit children. Perhaps it is one reason we thank Him for our blessings first when we pray—so we are continually reviewing what He has given us before we ask for more.

Young children often have this concept down. It makes me smile when my four year-old son thanks God in prayer for his bird pillow, his racecar blanket, his Mario game, and pizza ("Only pepperoni, not the other stuff"). Parents may be the official teachers, but I learn more about real gratitude from my preschooler than I could ever learn on my own.

A young friend who recently served in an orphanage in South America said that she was very affected by the orphans' prayers. While more fortunate kids may list their desires like a Christmas list, these faithful young people were thanking God for their running water and for a safe place to sleep. It also reminded me of my Romanian friends, who would give anything to enjoy the lifestyle we take for granted every day. Our immense blessings are almost incomprehensible to those in other parts of the world. I feel so blessed to live in this time and place. It makes me more determined not to take it for granted.

My Not-So-Big Trial

One of the greatest trials of my life was my parents' divorce. I was twenty-nine and married with three children, but it was still such a shock that it became all I could see for a while. We lived around the corner from my parents at the time, so it was hard to leave the house or even go to church without being confronted with the consequences of my parents' decision. Even their beautiful home, previously full of happy memories, suddenly felt like Ground Zero. My children's innocent inquiries of "Why don't Grandma and Grandpa live together anymore?" and "Will you and Daddy stop loving each other someday too?" brought forth a whole new wave of emotion.

Divorce rates are climbing, and unfortunately, it seems almost commonplace for many modern marriages to fail. Even television makes it seem like divorce isn't a big deal. But for me, the divorce rattled my spiritual foundation. It was a dark cloud hanging over my head for months. New developments—such as the daily "he said, she said" catastrophes and soap opera–like drama—kept the wound open for much longer than I should have allowed.

One day I had a conversation with my younger sister, Rachel, also married with three children. She had been struggling as well. She told me about a recent ladies' night with some friends.

"I looked around, and for the first time in a while, I really saw what these women were going through," she recalled. "One had just been through a horrible divorce and was suddenly a single parent. Another's husband had just lost his job and was concerned that they would lose their home. One woman had recently lost her husband to suicide. In an instant I was so grateful that my biggest trial was simply my parents' divorce!"

There is an old saying that if everyone set their troubles on a table, they would probably take back their own. This widening of focus to include everything we have been given, not just what we lack, has the power to change our entire outlook on life.

A Spirit of Thanksgiving

The happiest people I know have problems just like the rest of us. The difference is that these people are eternally grateful for their blessings. They see the positive about every negative. Some of it is genetics and how they were raised, but much of it is a personal decision.

A friend, mother of four, recently had a miscarriage. As she lay in bed, eyes puffy and red from crying, her seven-year-old daughter brought her some pancakes she had made herself. The girl asked what was wrong, and her mom told her as honestly as she could. Her daughter thought for a moment, then said, "Well, at least Heavenly Father has given you us, right?"

My friend chuckled as she told me, "What a great lesson on finding the positive—and from a seven-year-old!"

It is difficult to be grateful and grumpy at the same time. President Gordon B. Hinckley advised, "When you walk with gratitude, you do not walk with arrogance and conceit and egotism, you walk with a spirit of thanksgiving that is becoming to you and will bless your lives."[4]

The Divine Creator doesn't need our thanks. His role as Deity doesn't depend on our gratitude. He doesn't ask us to thank Him so He can feel like a good Father. He asks because He knows it changes us. It helps each of us get through our "tempest tossed" days. It gives what President Hinckley calls a "spirit of thanksgiving" that brings us one step closer to the Savior.

May we all take Bob's musical advice and count our blessings. I would love to say, to paraphrase a famous scripture, that "as for me and my house, we will thank the Lord." It may not abruptly change my life, but it will change my heart—and that's enough for me.

Notes

1. Henry B. Eyring, "Remembrance and Gratitude," *Ensign*, November 1989, 13.
2. Irving Berlin, "Count Your Blessings," *White Christmas*, 1954.
3. "Count Your Blessings," *Hymns*, 241.
4. Gordon B. Hinckley, *Teachings of Gordon B. Hinckley* (Salt Lake City: Deseret Book, 1997), 250.

19

Difficult Children

"And if those children are unresponsive, maybe you can't teach them yet, but you can love them. And if you love them today, maybe you can teach them tomorrow."

—Elder Jeffrey R. Holland[1]

IT'S HARD TO IMAGINE WHEN GAZING AT A TINY NEWBORN FACE that this infant could one day be a rebellious, angry teenager or an indifferent adult.

Some popular parenting books seem more like cookbooks. They seem to say that if we check off a specific list as that baby grows, our child is guaranteed to become what we want. So, like good mothers do, we pour every ingredient we have into the "pot"—including our own souls, it seems—to help our precious child come out just right. And yet, sometimes even after following the recipe precisely, it still doesn't turn out the way we'd hoped.

Expert Advice

While dealing with a difficult toddler a few years ago, I poured over those mainstream parenting books for months. Many focused on constant implementation of consequences, such as rewards and punishments. Others emphasized unconditional love and agency. Many of the books even seemed to contradict each other.

It wasn't until I threw out the expert advice and turned to the true Expert—the Father of countless billions of children—that my questions were finally answered. Our Father in Heaven is the ultimate parental example. Interestingly, He seems to prefer a gentle combination of both methods. He lays out the rules clearly, showering us with rewards and blessings when we obey, and letting us suffer the natural consequences when we don't.

But our Father also provides a merciful way out, or our own personal "get out of jail" card. He gives us a Savior. Surely when we go through the painful repentance process and allow Christ to take our burden, our Father rejoices. Surely He is truly joyful when His prodigal children return home.

Isn't it interesting that God gives us children of our own so unconditionally? He doesn't require us to take a written exam, proving that we know what we're doing. He doesn't ask for a childrearing résumé or an essay describing how His precious children will be protected from the world. He doesn't even give us a training manual. Our Father in Heaven knows that we aren't perfect and that parenthood means learning as we go. He knows that each of us is enough because we will rise to the challenge. We have spouses, friends, family, ward members, and medical professionals to assist us. But ultimately He wants us to turn to Him, the perfect parent, for advice.

Perhaps we are also meant to experience just a fraction of what He has experienced in parenthood. The complete and sudden sacrifice of bearing a child means at least eighteen (or thirty-five or sixty) years of stress, confusion, sorrow, stretching, soul-searching, and utter joy. Our children can be the cutest and most frustrating built-in trials in the world.

I love this quote by Elder Lynn G. Robbins:

> A sweet and obedient child will enroll a father or mother only in Parenting 101. If you are blessed with a child who tests your patience to the nth degree, you will be enrolled in Parenting 505. Rather than wonder what you might have done wrong in the premortal life to be so deserving, you might consider the more challenging child a blessing and opportunity to become more godlike yourself. With which child will your patience, long-suffering, and other Christlike virtues most likely be tested, developed, and refined? Could it be possible that you need this child as much as this child needs you?[2]

Rejection

One of the hardest things about having difficult children can be the rejection. A teenage daughter may roll her eyes at the reminder, but yes, her mother does remember changing her diapers and late-night feedings. And she clings to those memories of messy faces and "owies" and high fevers. No matter how self-sacrificing the mother, a child won't understand—at least, until she has children of her own. But it doesn't stop the mother from loving her child, does it?

Mothers aren't the only ones who experience constant rejection. We have numerous historical examples of heroic people who served others without knowing that their sacrifice would be accepted. Here we will look at three scripture stories, all with very different endings. As we read about them, though, we realize that each person had a very important part to play, regardless of what they may have thought at the time.

Abinadi was called to preach to the people of Noah. After being cast out, he returned again in disguise (what docs a Nephite disguise look like, I wonder?) and continued to deliver his message. The people hated him. The priests hated him. The king hated him. He probably died thinking that his words had fallen on deaf ears.

He did not see the fruits of his labor in this life. But because he persisted, we know that one priest was touched, and in turn an entire community of believers was born—as well as several generations of faithful followers (Mosiah 11–18).

The biblical Rebekah (a beautiful name, if I may say so) was an amazing woman. She is a great example of faith and dedicated motherhood. Julie Beck, former General Relief Society President, called her "one of the most pivotal and important people in the history of mankind, certainly in the house of Israel."[3] Rebekah's role was critical to the fulfilling of prophecy about the House of Israel and its future blessings. Sister Beck also said, "Those blessings are just now beginning to unfold after these many thousands of generations, but her blessings are happening in the world."[4] Her story occurred thousands of years ago, and yet her blessings are "just now beginning." It's possible that as Rebekah sorrowed over the contention between her twin sons, Jacob and Esau, she still didn't comprehend her importance in this life (Genesis 25:23). But her legacy has echoed over much of our history.

One of the best examples of rejection is Alma the Younger. After giving up the judgment seat for a higher purpose, he approached the wicked Nephite city of Ammonihah, "wrestling with God in mighty prayer, that he would pour out his Spirit upon the people who were in the city; that he would also grant that he might baptize them unto repentance" (Alma 8:10). How did the residents treat him after such sacrifice and genuine concern? To paraphrase, they retorted, "You gave up your leadership position, so you have no power over us." To put it in the words of my first grader, "You're not the boss of me!"

After being insulted, reviled, spit upon, and cast out of the city, Alma left with a heavy heart. We can only imagine that he was feeling partially responsible for the city's wickedness. He probably kicked himself for not giving up the judgment seat sooner, or for not checking up on the city before it had reached this point.

Suddenly an angel appeared and told him that he had "much cause to rejoice" because he had been faithful. Then the angel commanded him to return to Ammonihah and try again. Despite his traumatic first experience, Alma "returned speedily" to the city and entered "by another way" (Alma 8:12–18). It was there that he met Amulek, and you know the rest of his incredible story (Alma 8:10–27).

We sacrifice so much for our children, and sometimes it seems only to be thrown back in our faces. We harshly blame ourselves, asking ourselves where we went wrong with this child. And yet, as faithful mothers in Zion, we "enter the city" again and again, entering different ways each time, refusing to give up. We love our children too much to give up on them. That's why we're mothers.

Like the previous examples, we can't see the results of our labors yet either. Among us are thousands of modern-day heroic mothers who don't fully comprehend their importance right now. All we know is that watching someone we love struggle, and feeling powerless to help, is agonizingly hard.

What do we do then? We just keep trying. We love our children as our loving Father loves us, unconditionally and with an open heart. We love them as well as we can and leave the rest to their spiritual Parent—our Father in Heaven. We cling to every ounce of faith we have in our temple covenants and the promises we have received. Elder Orson F. Whitney's classic quote about temple covenants in a faithful family can soothe a worried mother's heart. He said: "Though some of the sheep may wander, the eye of the Shepherd is upon them, and sooner or later they will feel the tentacles of Divine Providence reaching out after them and drawing them back to the fold."[5]

Cookbooks can be wonderful guidelines as long as we remember that just as we have agency, so do our children. The recipe isn't flawed, and neither is the Master Chef. As the Chef's "assistants," we need to do what we can, let the rest go, and trust in His plan. And someday—hopefully sooner rather than later—we will finally see the rough ingredients simmer together into a culinary masterpiece.

Notes

1. Jeffrey R. Holland, "Teaching and Learning in the Church," *Ensign*, June 2007, 102.
2. Lynn G. Robbins, "What Manner of Men and Women Ought Ye To Be," *Ensign*, May 2011, 104.
3. Julie B. Beck, BYU Women's Conference, April 29, 2010.
4. Ibid.
5. Orson F. Whitney, in Conference Report, April 1929, 110; as quoted by Henry B. Eyring, "Our Perfect Example," *Ensign*, November 2009, 72.

20

We Are Not Alone

"Sometimes we make the mistake of feeling we are alone just because we are not getting recognition. Only a small part of what we do takes place in a public setting. The rest takes place in small and often unseen deeds. When you add the small deeds together, however, they are a thousand times greater than those receiving public recognition."

—Janette C. Hales[1]

"YOU'RE NOT ALONE." IT SOUNDS LIKE A NICE CHURCH SONG OR, on the other end of the spectrum, a quirky extra-terrestrial club theme. Yet how often we mothers need this reminder. Women in rural farming towns and single mothers may insist that they *are* alone, physically and emotionally. Mothers in crowded Los Angeles may feel isolated in what the world calls "old-fashioned" family ideals.

Elder Richard L. Evans said, "Loneliness is more than simply solitude. (A person can be very lonely in a crowded busy place.) And there is a kind of loneliness that comes from a sense of not belonging, of not fitting in, of not knowing our part in the picture."[2]

If not knowing our part in the picture is the malady, then perhaps knowing our part in the picture is the cure. C. S. Lewis said, "The homemaker has the ultimate career. All other careers exist to support the ultimate career."[3] Our work of raising children to God is among the highest duties a human being can possess. Yet, such a potentially isolating work requires that we have a network of support in a very unsupportive world.

Strands of Yarn

I love the yearly "unity" lesson in Relief Society. The teacher dutifully compares each of us to a piece of yarn. "Alone, we will break," she usually says. "But woven together, we are unbreakable." During a hard time in my life, I remember thinking, "That rope is doing great without me. Everyone else seems so much stronger. Why would they need one more insignificant piece of string?"

I didn't know my part in the picture. I didn't yet see the significance of a righteous mother. Moms, especially when they feel united in purpose, have a very real power. President Hinckley said that if we will be "united and speak with one voice, [our] strength will be incalculable."[4] And the Lord admonished, "be one, and if ye are not one ye are not mine" (Doctrine and Covenants 38:27). The fact that we aren't His if we are separated isn't necessarily a punishment, but rather a natural consequence.

It is so sad to hear women at church, a place of worship and the Lord's house, belittling each other because of their decisions or circumstances. Some mothers are required to support their families financially. Other mothers are able to stay home. Some mothers can't have children. Other mothers, in the eyes of their neighbors, have too many children! Our homes vary in taste and organization, and we all dress a little differently. We can't please everyone, nor should we try. The focus shouldn't be on making everyone the same, but rather learning from each other's unique approaches. No matter where we live or how strange our lifestyles may seem, we all have one very important thing in common: a testimony of the gospel with its ability to create eternal families.

Speaking about the stripling warriors' mothers, Julie Beck said,

"There wasn't one mother in that 2060 who was weak in her faith. It was the combination of the support they provided for each other and the help they gave to each other that made their homes unitedly powerful. That is what we provide for each other as sisters and daughters of God in the Lord's work."[5]

Angels Among Us

It's wonderful to feel that you are part of a larger purpose, isn't it? But how does it make you feel to hear that the Lord, Creator of the Universe, has made you this promise: "I will go before your face. I will be on your right hand and on your left, and my Spirit shall be in your hearts, and mine angels round about you, to bear you up" (Doctrine and Covenants 84:88). Are there really, as the song says, "angels among us?"

A wonderful example is the Old Testament story of Elisha and his servant. They were completely surrounded by the enemy's horses and chariots, and there seemed to be no hope. The servant said, "Alas, my master! How shall we do?" to which Elisha replied, "Fear not: for they that be with us, are more than they that be with them." Imagine the poor servant's expression as he stared at the enemy's army, thinking, *An army against two men, and he says there are more guys on our side than on theirs?* Then Elisha asked the Lord to "open his eyes, that he may see." Suddenly the servant saw what Elisha had seen: "the mountain was full of horses and chariots of fire round about Elisha" (2 Kings 6:15–17).

The amazing thing is that the Lord's promise is just as valid today. They may not appear in mass chariots, and they may not physically appear at all, but occasionally the veil can feel very thin.

One particular experience helped me catch the tiniest glimpse of the enormous support we have on the other side. It wasn't proof, by any means, that unseen spirits reside nearby. But for a lowly college sophomore, it was a personal confirmation that the Lord was mindful of me.

I had the opportunity to attend the Palmyra Temple dedication broadcast in the Marriott Center at BYU. The huge building that usually housed basketball games and graduation ceremonies suddenly became a hallowed place where Sunday dress and a special temple recommend were required. We sat quietly and reverently, watching our beloved prophet guide us through the dedication process. Suddenly, during the hymn, "The Spirit of God," I sat bolt upright in my seat. We were not alone, and I knew it. I saw dozens of heads throughout the room looking around and above us in wonder. Despite the many tens of thousands assembled in that large building, I could hear and feel a heavenly audience that had not been there before. I found tears streaming down my cheeks.

It's not a flowery concept, nor is it a strange one. We truly are not alone here on earth. President Ezra Taft Benson said that "If we only knew it, heavenly hosts are pulling for us—friends in heaven that we cannot now remember who yearn for our victory. This is our day to show what we can do—what life and sacrifice we can daily, hourly, instantly make for God. If we give our all, we will get His all from the greatest of all."[6]

When the house is a disaster area, our bodies ache with exhaustion, and it seems that no one else understands, it's hard to remember that we're part of a great work. But no mother is truly alone. We have other women in the church, we have friends and family on the other side of the veil, and we have our Heavenly Father. There truly are more on our side than on the side of the adversary. For "if God is for us, who can be against us?" (Romans 8:28–31).

Notes

1. Janette C. Hales, "You Are Not Alone," *Ensign*, May 1992, 80.

2. Richard L. Evans, *Conference Report*, October 1954, 86–89.
3. C.S. Lewis, as quoted by Richard and Linda Eyre, *Lifebalance* (New York: Random House, 1989), 84.
4. Gordon B. Hinckley, "Standing Strong and Immovable," Worldwide Leadership Training, January 2004, 20.
5. Julie B. Beck, BYU Women's Conference address, April 29, 2010.
6. Ezra Taft Benson, "Jesus Christ—Gifts and Expectations," *Ensign*, December 1988, 6.

21

The Empty Pitcher

"Traditionally we are taught, and instinctively we long, to give where it is needed—and immediately. Eternally, woman spills herself away in driblets to the thirsty, seldom being allowed the time, the quiet, the peace, to let the pitcher fill up to the brim."

—Anne Morrow Lindberg, author [1]

An old saying goes, "You can't fill a cup with an empty pitcher."

The pitcher of a mom's soul runs dry all too often. This book discusses some obvious refilling ideas—rest, play, positive thinking, gratitude, and playing with our kids. But one of the most devastating ways our pitcher can become empty is also the hardest to detect. If we aren't vigilant, motherhood can quickly drain us of our spiritual reserves. Between life's challenges, our own expectations, and the demands of children, even the best mother eventually "runs out," spiritually speaking.

At that point, we may keep trying to pour emptiness, analyzing the reasons why the pitcher isn't producing water. We wonder if the pitcher needs more time to accomplish all its demands, or if perhaps its expectations are too great. We coax and plead and order the empty pitcher to produce water. But there is only one way to refill the pitcher—from a source outside of ourselves.

There exists an unlimited source of pure, fresh, cool water from which can draw to nourish our families. The more we refill the pitcher at this source, the more we are able to share with those precious people in our lives. When daily activities prevent our own personal daily refill, the long-term effects can be damaging. We tell ourselves, "I am too busy to get a refill—I'll just have to go another day without water." We forget that often, when Mom's pitcher is empty, so are the cups of our children.

This source I'm referring to contains the purest, sweetest water that exists. It is inspiration and revelation from our Father in Heaven.

The best way I know to refill my pitcher at the source is what I call my "Triple Combination" time. It isn't the scripture set we carry around at church, but rather what our primary children call "Search, Ponder, and Pray," or scriptures, reflection, and prayer.

We tell ourselves, "I am too busy to get a refill—I'll just have to go another day without water." We forget that often, when Mom's pitcher is empty, so are the cups of our children.

Scriptures

The first part of this powerful combination is the scriptures. These sacred works impart much more than just the meaning of their words. They bring the Spirit into our hearts and homes. They answer troubling personal questions. They challenge us intellectually. They teach the mysteries of God as well as the simplest doctrine. They immerse us in a remembrance of what is most important. Scriptures focus our time and energy like nothing else can. President Kimball desired mothers to become "sister scriptorians."[2]

That's because we, in many ways, guide our families to what we feel is most important.

I love the levels of depth in each scripture story. The war chapters in Alma may seem a bit puzzling at times, but when I compare them to motherhood, everything suddenly makes sense. Even on the most basic level of understanding, raising children can feel like a battle every day. In fact, Ed Asner called motherhood "part joy, part guerilla warfare." There is a bit of truth to that, isn't there? In some ways we really are entering battle at the beginning of each day, and that battle is increasing in intensity and proximity.

In the great majority of earth's history, owning a set of scriptures would have been unheard of. Most people attended religious meetings at which they listened to sermons from a designated leader. That was life, and that was enough. But today's world is different, and as the challenges increase, so does our preparation. Today we are blessed to have scriptures in our home, in our own language, and we can read them whenever we want.

A favorite scripture story of mine is that of Helaman's warriors in Alma 56–58. It is often used on Mother's Day to show the value of a mother's teaching. But let's take it a step further. It's interesting that, while preparing their sons for war, these mothers were concerned that their sons had a strong spiritual foundation above all else. We can assume that these sons were eventually given a little physical training once they joined the army. But we know that it certainly wasn't their previous fighting skills that made them "firm and undaunted" and able to "administer death to all who opposed them" (Alma 57:19–20). They had been raised to avoid such things, in fact. The training they had received was spiritual training. Their mothers were more concerned about filling their sons' cups than about training them in physical combat. These women probably did not have scriptures in their homes. But if they were living today, I'd bet that they would be "sister scriptorians"!

Pondering

Simply reading the scriptures is not enough. We need to digest what we are reading, to absorb the parts that strike us as applicable in our own lives. I have found that no matter how many times I read the Book of Mormon, I notice something new each time. A certain passage will take hold of my mind, and I'll sit back and think about it for a while. It is in those quiet moments, when my mind is unoccupied and my heart is open, that inspiration comes. Somehow those moments of reflection fill my soul so thoroughly that I can't contain the flood of pure understanding. Such peace helps me prepare for the demanding day ahead.

During the Savior's forty-day fast before his ministry officially began, he initiated some personal preparation time as well. Joseph B. Wirthlin said: "It is in solitude, pondering, and praying that Jesus made ready to battle Satan face-to-face and resist and overcome all of his enticements. . . . It is only in solitude, pondering, and meditating that we live in closest relationship with our Lord."[3]

Even people who are not of our faith recognize the rejuvenating effects of a little quiet time each day. These effects are particularly important for women. Barbara DeAngelis, a relationships expert, said, "Women need real moments of solitude and self-reflection to balance out how much of ourselves we give away."[4]

Whether it lasts twenty minutes or twenty seconds, this sacred time of reflection has a very real power. And when combined with the other two parts of the Triple Combination, it can truly overflow a mother's spiritual pitcher.

Prayer

This aspect of the Triple Combination is so important that the entire next chapter is dedicated to it. But we do know that communicating with our Father in Heaven, when combined with reading

His word and listening to His Spirit, is a blessing that too few in the history of the earth have enjoyed.

Triple Combination time has the power to change an entire day. When I skip that time, not only do I miss out on the power it could have bestowed, but the day just feels a little off. Things just don't seem quite right. In the words of a former Mia Maid leader, "When I forget my scriptures and prayer in the morning, I feel like I've forgotten to put on my bra!"

Find your own Triple Combination time. Not only will you feel better about yourself and your day, but your children's cups will increase in capacity as well. Elder M. Russell Ballard said, "Organize your personal lives to provide time for prayer and scriptures. . . . Teach [your children] that living the gospel will lead them away from the filth, promiscuity, and violence of the Internet, media, and video games. They will not be lost, and they will be prepared to handle responsibility when it is thrust upon them."[5]

We should consider Triple Combination time to be our own personal meditation time, our own refilling station. This is our time to connect with our Father. This is *our* time.

Let's immerse ourselves, if only for five minutes. We can't let our children, our spouses, our Facebook friends, or anyone else make this decision for us. We should consider Triple Combination time to be our own personal meditation time, our own refilling station. This is our time to connect with our Father. This is *our* time. It's an indulgence we can't afford to skip. So let's sneak some of the kids' Easter candy (without them seeing, of course) or a bag of M&Ms. We can tell the children we are doing some therapy and retreat to the bedroom. It may help to play soft, inspiring music to drown out the background noise (or better yet, get up early). It may also help to write our thoughts in a journal. Let's carve out this special time and feel the pitcher become full to overflowing.

When we take the time for a daily refill, we are much more prepared for the endless demands placed upon us. And when our children's cups eventually run dry, our freshly refilled pitchers will be ready to save the day.

Notes

1. Anne Morrow Lindbergh, *Gift From the Sea* (New York: Pantheon Books, 1975), 39.
2. Spencer W. Kimball, "The Role of Righteous Women," *Ensign*, November 1979, 103–4.
3. Joseph B. Wirthlin, *Finding Peace in Our Lives* (Salt Lake City: Deseret Book, 1995), 37.
4. Barbara DeAngelis, PhD, *Real Moments: Discover the Secret for True Happiness* (New York: Random House, 1995), 177.
5. M. Russell Ballard, "That the Lost May Be Found," *Ensign*, May 2012, 99.

22

The Gift of Prayer

"When I was a little child, my parents taught me by example to pray. I began with a picture in my mind of Heavenly Father being far away. As I have matured, my experience with prayer has changed. The picture in my mind has become one of a Heavenly Father who is close by, who is bathed in a bright light, and who knows me perfectly."

—President Henry B. Eyring [1]

I LOVE TO TRAVEL. THERE IS SOMETHING SO HUMBLING ABOUT immersing myself in a different way of life. I've had the amazing opportunity to visit eleven European countries as well as Canada and Mexico, and each one has introduced a whole new perspective on life. I would trade it all, though, for the chance to go to Israel. Imagine walking in the very place where Christ, Savior of worlds, spent His mortality. It sounds like an incredible experience.

Those who have been to Jerusalem have probably visited the "Western Wall," sometimes called the "Wailing Wall." Jews believe that the wall is the last remnant of the ancient temple. They visit the wall frequently to pray, often writing their prayers on slips of paper and sticking them between the stones. The belief is that this method will get their prayers to heaven more surely than anywhere else—or in other words, it's the closest to the One God that they can get.

Contrast that belief with a religion that believes even a toddler can speak directly to God, anytime, anywhere. This belief in God as our loving Father is actually quite strange to many other faiths. We don't realize how unique that position is. And yet, when reading the New Testament, it's hard to come to any other conclusion about the nature of Deity. This Church is true, and regular communication with God for *everyone* is at the center of it.

As If He Were Present

George Albert Smith recalled the story of a nine-year-old orphan boy who had been living with friends. The boy became very sick, was rushed to the hospital, and was told that surgery was needed immediately. While the doctors and nurses prepared to operate, the boy asked one of the doctors if he would pray for him. The doctor said he could not. The boy then asked the other members of the medical staff around him, and each one uncomfortably declined.

Finally, something very remarkable happened; this little fellow said, "If you can't pray for me, will you please wait while I pray for myself?" They removed the sheet, and he knelt on the operating table, bowed his head, and said, "Heavenly Father, I am only an orphan boy. I am awful sick. Won't you please make me well? Bless these men who are going to operate that they will do it right. If you will make me well, I will try to grow up to be a good man. Thank you, Heavenly Father, for making me well." When he got through praying, he lay down. The doctors' and the nurses' eyes were filled with tears. Then he said, "I am ready." The operation was performed. The little fellow was taken back to his room, and in a few days they took him from the hospital, well on the way to a complete recovery.

> When later asked about the surgery by an inquirer, one of the surgeons said, "I have operated on hundreds of people, men and women who thought they had faith to be healed; but never until I stood over that little boy have I felt the presence

> of God as I felt it then. That boy opened the windows of heaven and talked to his Heavenly Father as one would talk to another face to face. I want to say to you that I am a better man for having had this experience of standing and hearing a little boy talk to his Father in Heaven as if he were present."[2]

There is something so pure about hearing the prayer of a child. Kids haven't been tainted yet by the world's idea of God being unreachably distant. They have an untarnished testimony that if they ask, they shall receive (3 Nephi 27:29). So they ask. They may ask for a new Tonka truck or for a younger sister to move to the zoo, but they will still ask! Some of the most touching prayers I have ever heard have come from children.

Joseph Smith was only fourteen years old when he had his remarkable vision. Perhaps it is Joseph Smith's childlike faith that allowed him to have such a sacred experience. He had been promised that if he had a question, he could pray and the answer would be given to him (James 1:5). So he asked, he received, and the remarkable exchange officially reopened the doors of revelation from God to His children.

And yet, sometimes it's easy to overlook the fact that we can communicate with the Father just as Joseph did. The praying process is the same for the prophet as it is for a toddler. President Henry B. Eyring said, "He hears our prayers as He heard Joseph's prayer—as clearly as if they were being offered in His presence."[3]

The Power of Prayer

I love this Church because it confirms my feelings about prayer. I know that God lives because of prayer. Not only has He given me a testimony of the gospel though prayer, but He has answered numerous heartfelt supplications in a way that left me with no doubt of His existence.

I remember once as a young girl playing with a neighbor friend and getting injured. I couldn't stand up, much less walk home, and there were no adults nearby. So I said a simple prayer: "Heavenly Father, I'm hurt and I can't get home. Please tell my mom to come find me."

It was a couple minutes before she arrived, breathless and concerned. "Did something happen? I suddenly felt like I needed to come check on you!"

Grinning knowingly, my mischievous little girl self asked, "What took you so long?"

Most mothers already have a testimony of prayer. We have seen its power in our lives, and we want it to be a major part of our children's lives as well. But sometimes the light of our testimonies gets lost in translation. Perhaps the first step to teaching our kids about prayer is simply to pray.

We say a lot of prayers in the gospel. With personal prayers, family prayers, blessings on meals, and prayers at church, a Latter-day Saint child can participate in about fifty-three prayers a week. That totals almost fifty thousand prayers before she leaves for college. If that doesn't start a habit of communication with God, there's not much else that will. And imagine the peaceful spirit in a home where continual prayer is a regular companion.

Perhaps the first step to teaching our kids about prayer is simply to pray.

Once the habit of prayer is firmly established, we can continually work on the quality and meaning of our prayers. It is especially helpful to do this with our children. What an honor it is to share our testimonies of literal communication with God to our families.

President George Albert Smith told the story of how he was

taught to pray by his mother. She showed him how to kneel by his trundle bed, folded his little hands, and taught him his first prayer. "It was such a simple prayer, but . . . that prayer opened for me the windows of heaven," he recalled. "From that day until now . . . wherever I have been, when I have gone to my bed or arisen from it, I have felt I was close to my Heavenly Father. He is not far away."[4]

Prayer is powerful. It brings the Spirit into our homes. It opens our hearts and helps us receive messages from our all-knowing Father. It helps us thank Him for our incomprehensible blessings. It gives us a way to ask for things we could never achieve or obtain by ourselves. It sets an example for our children. And best of all, prayer is for everyone—children, adults, politicians, movie stars, church leaders, criminals, members of other faiths, and even the resurrected Christ (3 Nephi 17:14–18). We are all invited to communicate with the all-knowing Creator of the universe.

What an incredible privilege.

Notes

1. Henry B. Eyring, "Exhort Them to Pray," *Ensign*, February 2012, 4.
2. George Albert Smith, *Teachings of Presidents of the Church: George Albert Smith* (Salt Lake City: Intellectual Reserve, 2011), 95–96.
3. Henry B. Eyring, "Exhort Them to Pray," *Ensign*, February 2012, 4.
4. George Albert Smith, *Teachings of Presidents of the Church: George Albert Smith* (Salt Lake City: Intellectual Reserve, 2011) 93–94.

23

The Definition of Integrity

"Never let failure progress from an action to an identity."

—Carol Dweck, PhD [1]

THE YOUNG WOMEN PROGRAM IS POWERFUL. THERE IS PROfound wisdom in the theme our girls repeat each Sunday. My favorite Young Women value was always integrity. It seemed to encompass all the other values (not to mention that its color, purple, was my favorite). The Young Women materials define integrity as "the moral courage to make our actions consistent with our knowledge of right and wrong."[2]

In other words, integrity is doing what we believe, and being what we say we are. There is no disconnection between the outside (actions) and the inside (beliefs), or between the "Do's" and the "Be's."

The Savior asked the Nephites a powerful question: "What manner of men [and women] ought ye to be? Verily I say unto you, even as I am" (3 Nephi 27:27).

Elder Lynn G. Robbins pointed out that to be like Christ, we have to do the things that Christ did. He also made the point that one cannot exist without the other—actions and beliefs have to be consistent with one another. The Savior condemned hypocrites for doing good without being good (Mark 7:6), but we also learn that faith without works is dead (James 2:17). Elder Robbins remarked, "Do without be—hypocrisy—portrays a false image to others, while be without do portrays a false image to oneself."[3]

Elder Robbins's talk has made me ask some tough questions: Am I doing without being? Is the *appearance* more important than the actual *being* for me?

My husband always teases me about being late for church. I tell myself that it's always the last minute shoe-searching and snack-bagging that gets us there late. But inside, I know the truth. I probably put more emphasis on my family looking perfect than I do on being on time to church. If my kids don't arrive ready for a model shoot, we have fallen short. We should look our best in the Lord's house, of course. But I think the Lord would forgive my daughter for not wearing the right color hair bow and overlook my son's mismatched socks. I think He would rather that I emphasize worshiping Him on Sunday than worshiping compliments on how adorable my children look. It's a disconnect between my beliefs and my actions. It's something I need to change.

Teaching Our Children

What does this mean for mothers? Elder Robbins continued:

> Because *be* begets *do* and is the motive behind *do*, teaching *be* will improve behavior more effectively than focusing on *do* will improve behavior. When children misbehave . . . we often misdirect our discipline on what they *did*. . . . But the *do*—their behavior—is only a symptom of the unseen motive in their hearts. We might ask ourselves, "What attributes, if understood by the child, would correct this behavior in the

future? Being patient and forgiving when annoyed? Loving and being a peacemaker? Taking personal responsibility for one's actions and not blaming?"[4]

This is what mothers do. We are much more than babysitters and cooks, house-cleaners and providers. Our actions and our roles are in helping our children lay the foundations for their own futures. We are teaching math to future physicists and spelling to future teachers. We are teaching them doing and being and becoming. We are showing them integrity. We hold precious lives in our hands—souls that are not truly ours, but God's. What an incredible job we have, you and I!

And yet, we have to be so careful with that responsibility.

Our actions and our roles are in helping our children lay the foundations for their own futures. We are teaching them doing and being and becoming. We are showing them integrity.

"*Discipline*," Elder Robbins continued, "comes from the same root word as *disciple* and implies patience and teaching on our part."[5]

Rather than harsh punishment, this teaching should be a gentle lesson of consequences, using persuasion, long-suffering, gentleness and meekness, love unfeigned, kindness, and pure knowledge (Doctrine and Covenants 121:41–42). This type of teaching is tough. It requires patience and a humble heart to listen to the Spirit when opportunities for lessons arise.

But the most important lesson should be that what our children do isn't more important than who they are. Even the most disobedient child's worth is beyond that of worlds. Conversely, even the most obedient child can end up an overstrung, anxious valedictorian if she believes her worth is based on her achievements. We praise our kids for getting good grades and practicing the piano and scoring runs in baseball. But are we pleased with the people that they are becoming?

And if so, do they know it?

Mothering with Integrity

There's a law of nature that I sometimes wish could be changed. The law is that animals create other animals like themselves. Frogs don't give birth to zebras. They give birth to tadpoles. Horses don't have kittens, but foals. Human mothers have human children, and chances are that they will turn out much like their parents. (Do you ever find words coming out of your mouth that sound just like your mother? It's a blessing and a curse.)

To be fair, humans are a bit different than animals (some of us more than others). We have the power to decide what *type* of human we will be. Our children have the ability to overcome a difficult childhood and excel. They also have the agency to override a fantastic childhood and make poor decisions (just ask Lehi and Sariah). But for the most part, children become much like their parents.

One reason for this is that they learn by example. Research has shown that fathers who smoke cigarettes are much more likely to have children who smoke. Mothers who stay physically fit are more likely to have children who are fit. And most important, parents who put God first in their own lives are more likely to have children who do so as well.

If I ever start to stray from the gospel or become indifferent, I will re-read Elder Holland's talk, "A Prayer for the Children." He said:

> Parents simply cannot flirt with skepticism or cynicism, then be surprised when their children expand that flirtation into

> full-blown romance. If in matters of faith and belief children are at risk of being swept downstream by this intellectual current or that cultural rapid, we as their parents must be more certain than ever to hold to anchored, unmistakable moorings clearly recognizable to those of our own household. It won't help anyone if we go over the edge with them, explaining through the roar of the falls all the way down that we really did know the Church was true but we just didn't want to stifle anyone's freedom to think otherwise. No, we can hardly expect the children to get to shore safely if the parents don't seem to know where to anchor their own boat.[6]

It may be a harsh rule of nature, but it's also one of the most fantastic challenges of motherhood: We have to be what we want our children to be. We have to do what we want our children to do. We are the teachers of integrity. We are helping each other make it back to our Heavenly Father. We help our children, but our children also help us. The hearts of the children turn to the fathers, and the hearts of the fathers to their children (Malachi 4:6). We are all in this together. That's the purpose of a family.

In the process of keeping our actions consistent with our knowledge of right and wrong, we will ultimately find more peace. Any discord within will fade to a gentle hum of harmony between who we are and how we act. And hopefully we will become that much more like our ultimate example, the Savior.

Notes

1. Carol Dweck, quoted in Joe Kita, "Bounce Back Chronicles," *Reader's Digest*, May 2009, 95.
2. Personal Progress, The Church of Jesus Christ of Latter-day Saints, https://www.lds.org/young-women/personal-progress/integrity?lang=eng.

3. Lynn G. Robbins, "What Manner of Men and Women Ought Ye to Be?" *Ensign*, May 2011, 103.
4. Ibid.
5. Ibid., 104.
6. Jeffrey R. Holland, "A Prayer for the Children," *Ensign*, May 2003, 86.

24

The Super Woman

"My idea of superwoman is someone who scrubs her own floors."

—Bette Midler [1]

WOULDN'T IT BE WONDERFUL TO HAVE SUPER POWERS? IF only we could don a special cape that allowed us to sprout two more arms or even a personal helper clone for the day.

Sister Elaine L. Jack, a former Relief Society president, said:

> For thirty years I have wanted to meet the woman against whom more Latter-day Saint women have compared themselves than any other woman in the Church. She's often thought of as "Superwoman." Some call her the typical Relief Society sister, the woman who makes fabulous bread, plays the organ like a professional, and dresses her impeccably groomed children in the clothes she's made. Who is she? What does she do that makes her seem beyond the reach of any woman? I've made a careful study, and I've found this woman. . . . The good news is that she actually does exist. The better news is that she is wonderful. The best news is that she's you! And this is who you really are! [2]

When I first read this quote, I thought, "Thanks, but I'm no Superwoman. I definitely don't fit that description." But the more I thought about it, the more I realized something. It doesn't matter if I can't soar into the sunset or play the organ in church or even sew a straight line. That's not in my job description anyway. My job is not to be Superwoman, who can do all things perfectly and save the day, but rather a Super Woman. I just need to be the best me I can be.

At first it sounds like a second-grade self-esteem campaign motto. Yes, we do need to be the best we can be. We Latter-day Saint moms have more expected of us than most mothers, it's true. But we also have the tools to fulfill those expectations. We have modern-day revelation, scriptures, Relief Society and other Church programs, and one especially helpful tool: the Spirit of God.

The Spirit: A Super Woman's Gift

The Holy Ghost can be the most powerful gift we have here in mortality. It may seem much like a superpower to those who haven't experienced it. The Spirit can help us know what to say in a difficult moment. We can be warned of danger. The Spirit whispers when our children are in trouble or making trouble or about to get *into* trouble. LDS mothers have a gift from God Himself. We have the Holy Ghost.

The Spirit, as the third member of the Godhead, can be with us all the time. In fact, he never leaves unless we drive him away. But too often we try to plug away on our own, day after day, refusing to use that special power. The Spirit is a gift and a blessing, but we sometimes forget the very real power it can have on our homes and families.

President Brigham Young said: "There is no doubt, if a person lives according to the revelations given to God's people, he may have the Spirit of the Lord to signify to him His will, and to guide and to direct him in the discharge of his duties, in his temporal as well as his spiritual exercises. I am satisfied, however, that in this respect, we live far beneath our privileges."[3]

A Super Woman doesn't need to save the world. She just needs to follow those gentle promptings that guide those in her stewardship. The Spirit helps us become better teachers to our children. The Spirit can use us to answer the prayers of others. The Spirit encourages us to be just a bit better, or even warns us of impending danger. A Super Woman has learned from past experience to pay attention to those feelings.

Do you remember your first experience with the Holy Ghost? I don't remember mine, but I do remember a story my mother told me.

She had just been baptized and confirmed. She and her brothers were playing tag barefoot in the yard. One brother turned to chase her. Not to be outdone by her younger sibling, she started to run across some ivy to safety. As she stepped into the prickly leaves, a distinct voice said, "Don't run in that ivy." She stopped, unsure, but shrugged it off and leaped forward. In an instant a searing pain tore across her bare foot. She had sliced it open on a hidden piece of glass. Dozens of stitches later, she realized that the still small voice she had heard was the Spirit. In the years that followed, my mother was diligent to always listen to that voice as she raised her children. Her example had a profound effect on her daughters.

A Super Woman doesn't need to save the world. She just needs to follow those gentle promptings that guide those in her stewardship.

Having the Holy Ghost with Us Always

How can we have the Spirit with us at all times? Do we have to be living perfect lives, with perfect children in tow, in order to receive this wonderful gift? No. Actually, the key to having the

Holy Ghost with us always is nothing mysterious; it is recited every Sunday during the sacrament prayer.

If we 1) take upon us the name of Christ, 2) always remember Him, and 3) keep His commandments, we may always have His Spirit to be with us (Doctrine and Covenants 20:77, Moroni 4:3). To me, these three points reflect a lifestyle of commitment to the gospel and to Christ more than a rigid set of unreachable requirements. If we are consistently trying our best, we can have the Spirit with us. And when we have the Spirit with us, our best will become even better. Only then will we be able to live "within our privileges" as Brigham Young counseled.

Those who criticize us for trying to accomplish too much as members of the Church don't understand one very important thing: "Whom the Lord calls, the Lord qualifies."[4] He expects a lot from mothers, but He also gives us the means by which we can accomplish it. He doesn't give us four arms or clones because He knows we *can* do it with the help of His Spirit, and we do it every day.

We can't afford to lose the warmth of the Holy Ghost. Our children are too valuable, our families too precious. We can't go a single morning without praying for that protection to be with us.

One afternoon I left my husband and young children in the backyard and climbed into our SUV to run an errand. As I pulled into reverse, I felt a small voice say, "Look behind the car." I stopped for a moment. The kids couldn't have climbed the fence to the front yard, and they couldn't have come through the house that quickly. There was no reason why I should stop, unbuckle my seat belt, and walk to the back of the car. I didn't even see anything in the rearview mirror.

But then the voice came again. "Look behind the car."

I pulled into park, slid out of the car, and walked around. Then my breath caught. My two-year-old nephew, who lived next door, was just crossing the driveway. He held a worn blanket in one hand

and a bottle in the other. He had escaped his house undiscovered at naptime. More importantly, he would have walked behind the car just as I pulled out. Now I try to listen for that still, small voice more carefully. It is indeed a powerful gift.

The Danger of Comparison

It's hard for the Holy Ghost to remain with us when we are critical and harsh on ourselves. We need to stop comparing ourselves to the seeming Superwomen around us and become the best Super Women we can become.

As Elder Marvin J. Ashton said:

> Many [women] seem to put too much pressure on themselves to be a "supermom" or "superwoman." Sisters, do not allow yourselves to be made to feel inadequate or frustrated because you cannot do everything others seem to be accomplishing. Each should assess her own situation, her own energy, and her own talents, and then choose the best way to mold her family into a team, a unit that works together and supports each other.[5]

The best superheroes, I would assume, know how to gather their assets and make a plan of action. I am constantly asking myself which changes we can make to help the Spirit be more influential in our home. The Holy Ghost is helpful to me, true, but also to my children. I want them to get used to that warm feeling so they don't want it to leave.

Isn't it amazing? The Supreme Being of the universe has given us His Spirit to be with us always. I don't know of any gift He could have given me that would be more helpful as I raise my kids (although at times a second set of arms *would* be pretty helpful). He knows these children even better than I do. They belong to Him more than they belong to me. He also wants them to return to

Him. Of course He would bestow His Spirit to help guide a struggling mother in the greatest work ever performed—child rearing.

Let's put on our capes, Super Women. We are well equipped, and we are ready. Let's go make our homes a little better. Hopefully it will help our children turn out to be Super Children, and ultimately Super Parents themselves.

Notes

1. Attributed to Bette Midler, weightwatchers.com/util/art/index_art.aspx?tabnum=1&art_id=732218.sc=4394.
2. Elaine L. Jack, "These Things Are Manifested Unto Us Plainly," *Ensign*, October 1990, 88–90.
3. Brigham Young, *Journal of Discourses* 12 (London: Latter-day Saint's Book Depot, 1869), 104.
4. Ibid.
5. Marvin J. Ashton, "Choose the Good Part," *Ensign*, May 1984, 10.

Puzzle Piece #5

Mother of Wisdom

A mother of wisdom resists comparison and is content with her blessings. She has patience in obtaining the things that are important to her. She refuses to buy into the world's views of body image and varying worth. She is determined to stand for truth and righteousness when society flaunts immorality and moral indecisiveness.

25

"The Grass Is Greener" Syndrome

"I want my children to have all the things I couldn't afford. Then I want to move in with them."

—Phyllis Diller, comedienne[1]

I REMEMBER AN EFY TALK YEARS AGO (NOT THAT LONG AGO) IN which the speaker's main point was that our bodies have appetites and desires that need to be controlled, and that they take a lifetime to master.

Mosiah 3:19 says that "the natural man [and woman] is an enemy to God, and has been from the fall of Adam, and will be, forever and ever, unless he [or she] yields to the enticings of the Holy Spirit, and putteth off the natural man [or woman] and becometh a saint through the atonement of Christ the Lord."

Our carnal nature is often so ingrained that "natural" is indeed a good way to describe it. And much of that carnal nature consists of legitimate physical needs, such as sleep, nourishment, affection, and more. These are genuine needs. We couldn't survive without them.

However, we have power to overcome those needs when a situation requires it, however temporarily. We go without food for two meals on fast Sundays, wielding power over our bodies for a higher purpose. Mothers sacrifice sleep for their young children. Single mothers (and sometimes, sadly, even married ones) who starve painfully for affection from a spouse pour love into their children instead. These women constantly scrape the inner barrels of strength, choosing to try when they want nothing more than to give up. There is such nobility in the human spirit.

Other carnal desires are less black-and-white. These universal appetites are more difficult to overcome. One of the most unforgiving appetites is what some call "Grass is Greener" syndrome. The natural woman inside each of us likes to compare herself to others. She thinks, *The neighbors have a shiny new camper—why don't we get one?* Or, *Sister So-and-so's kids always look so put-together at church. We need to start shopping at Dillard's.* Or even, *The neighbor's wood floors are so much nicer than our ugly ceramic tile!* (That one is my weakness.)

Chances are, even if we did shop at Dillard's and buy a new camper and lay down expensive wood floors, we would still be unfulfilled. Other people's grass would still be greener than ours because there will always be families with more money or better-behaved children or three-year-old piano prodigies when our kids refuse to practice at all. There will always be nicer yards and more expensive cars and better jobs. The point here isn't in reaching that unattainable goal of better or more, but rather where we pour our precious energy and time.

Nephi's younger brother Jacob said, "Wherefore, do not spend money for that which is of no worth, nor your labor for that which cannot satisfy. Hearken diligently unto me, and remember the words which I have spoken; and come unto the Holy One of Israel, and feast upon that which perisheth not, neither can be corrupted, and let your soul delight in fatness" (2 Nephi 9:51).

The Need for Fulfillment

A classic movie, *Chariots of Fire*, tells the story of two young runners. Eric Liddell is a Scottish Christian who wants to use his running talent to further the kingdom of God. Harold Abrahams is an English Jew who simply wants to beat everyone else so he can be the best, which he believes will satisfy his hunger for vengeance against a prejudiced world. (The particular religions aren't necessarily the point, however. The tables could easily have been turned, with a bitter Christian man versus a Jew trying to honor God instead.) Eventually they both make it to the Olympics. Liddell accomplishes his goal and glorifies God. Abrahams also wins, but something interesting happens—he feels more empty than before. He has achieved his ultimate life's dream, only to find that it doesn't make him feel any more fulfilled.[2] He has been chasing a dream that evaporated when he finally obtained it.

It is a good lesson for all of us. As mothers well know, true happiness is usually found outside of ourselves and our own wants.

Financial Fulfillment

It's a fine line to decide where to put our focus. There are dozens of ways to spend our hard-earned money. Sometimes we feel as though it is gone before we even see it.

One of the biggest challenges for families today is simply making ends meet financially. Parents struggle with falling home values, unemployment, and skyrocketing prices. It's more important now than ever before to search our hearts (and wallets) to decide what is critical and what is optional in our family's budget.

Elder Ballard said:

> Through wise budgeting, control your real needs and measure them carefully against your many wants in life. Far too many individuals and families have incurred too much debt. Be

> careful of the many attractive offers to borrow money. It is much easier to borrow money than it is to pay it back. There are no shortcuts to financial security. There are no get-rich-quick schemes that work. Perhaps none need the principle of balance in their lives more than those who are driven toward accumulating "things" in this world. [3]

A few minutes in front of the TV or listening to commercials on the radio (does anyone listen to commercials anymore?) are very illuminating. The world likes to advertise two very convincing ideas: 1) That we are entitled to a life of luxury and ease because we "deserve" it, and 2) We don't need to wait for the things that we want. The days of saving pennies in a jar for a big purchase seem to be long gone—a swipe of a plastic card, and it's ours. It's all too easy to have whatever we desire right away. And if fighting entitlement is that difficult now, imagine the chaotic world our children will be living in.

Where to Invest

A few years ago we met an extraordinary family. The children—six of them, ranging in age from twenty-two to seven—simply stood out because of their enthusiasm for life. Even the younger ones radiated with the light of the gospel. I asked the mother, Jen, for her secret.

"We decided in the beginning to invest in experiences, not things," she said simply.

Jen then explained that she had been expecting their fourth child at the time of this decision. They had recently bought a house and were on their way to being financially stable for the first time in their eight-year marriage. Then she had a unique opportunity to receive a priesthood blessing from their bishop.

Her blessing consisted of several thoughtful promises, but one in particular made her heart sink. "He said, 'I bless you to never be rich,'" she recalled. "I remember thinking, is that a blessing? And then he said that, nevertheless, we would have sufficient for our needs."

At first, Jen was troubled. But as time went on, she realized what a blessing that promise truly was. By removing wealth as an option, they could decide how else to spend their energy. She and her husband chose to invest in their childrens' growth, including music lessons, sports, and outdoor activities. They decided that it was more important to build their children's self-confidence and sense of responsibility than to have expensive vacations and toys.

Their effort seems to have paid off. They currently have two missionaries in the field, and two of their children have served in student government at school. They are talented athletes or musicians and enthusiastic church-goers. But most importantly, their focus is on things that "perisheth not, neither can be corrupted" (2 Nephi 9:51).

Materialism is an unforgiving taskmaster. Once we buy in, we are entering a bottomless chasm of jealousy, entitlement, and endless comparison. I've found myself stuck in that cycle before, and I simply couldn't find peace. I was ever chasing a dream that never quite materialized.

Matthew 6:24 says that "No [woman] can serve two masters: for either [she] will hate the one, and love the other; or else [she] will hold to the one, and despise the other. Ye cannot serve God and mammon." We all decide which side we will serve. We need to make the decision, then remake it, then make it again. But the rewards are far greater when we make God our master. He rewards our service with the promise, "I will pour out my Spirit upon you, and great shall be your blessing—yea, even more than if you should obtain treasures of earth and corruptibleness to the extent thereof" (Doctrine and Covenants 19:38).

Peace lies in being content with what we have, not in crossing over to the neighbors' greener grass. I love the saying, "The grass isn't greener on the other side. The grass is greener where you water it!"

Let's find a bucket and go to work.

Notes

1. Phyllis Diller, as quoted by Tom Corr, *The 2320 Funniest Quotes* (Berkeley: Ulysses Press, 2011), 84.
2. *Chariots of Fire*, 1981. Written by Colin Welland, directed by Hugh Hudson.
3. M. Russell Ballard, "Keeping Life's Demands in Balance," *Ensign*, May 1987, 14.

26

Waiting for Marshmallows

"Self-control is one mark of a mature person; it applies to control of language, physical treatment of others, and the appetites of the body."

—Elder Joseph B. Wirthlin [1]

IF YOU'VE STUDIED PSYCHOLOGY OR CHILD DEVELOPMENT, YOU'VE probably heard of the Stanford marshmallow experiment (Mischel, 1972). A researcher would take a child aged four to six to an empty room, set a tray with a marshmallow in front of him, and say, "If you wait to eat this until I get back, you can have *two* marshmallows." Then the researcher left.

I often wonder what my own children would have done. Of course, some of the children ate the marshmallow as soon as the door closed. Most of the six hundred kids tried to wait but gave up after an average of three minutes. But remarkably, about 30 percent of the kids held out for the second marshmallow. How did they do it? They used tactics such as covering their eyes, turning away to avoid looking at their temptation, and even playing with the marshmallow like a small pet.

The study wasn't intended to torture children, however. The researchers wanted to know what these kids' ability to wait meant for them later in life. As the children reached adolescence, those who had deferred gratification had higher SAT scores and were considered "significantly more competent" than those who hadn't waited. The correlation between the child's ability to prolong gratification and his later success was astounding.[2]

As mothers, we know that patience is a good habit for our children to develop. We are constantly telling our children to wait. See if any of the following sounds familiar:

- "Be patient! Dinner is almost ready."
- "No, you cannot have ice cream right now. It's time for bed."
- "No, you may not drive the family car. You're twelve. Wait until you're sixteen."
- "Wait until your homework is done before you play with your friends."

Mothers instinctively know that making our kids wait for something they want is a good tactic. It teaches them patience. It slows them down a bit, helps them focus, and makes them prioritize. One thing we may overlook is that our example teaches the strongest lesson of all.

We recently moved to a new house (again). This time, we had a little money saved to do some remodeling. We laid new wood floors (much better than dirty tile, right?) and new carpet, painted the walls, bought some new furniture—and promptly ran out of money.

My dear husband was fine with that. We had done so much that he was content with the house being the way it was. After all, it looked much better than when we had moved in. But unfortunately, the natural woman (and the home decorator) in me was screaming,

"It's so close! If we could just finish painting the rest of the house and put a fence in the backyard, then I could be happy."

We had a decision to make. Did we save up over a period of several months? Or did we whip out the credit card, ignore the high interest rate, and have it now? For my husband, it was an easy decision. For me, it was really hard. But we eventually decided to save up for the rest of the projects.

That would be a sweet little ending to the story except for one thing. When we had finally saved enough to begin work again the next spring, guess what happened? Taxes. We had neglected to save enough to cover an untaxed portion of my husband's income, and before we knew it, the money was gone again. All of it. Time for another decision.

Unfortunately, there will always be financial decisions. A daughter will need braces. A son will total the car (hopefully not at age twelve). The townhouse will always need to be fixed somewhere. A sick family member will need surgery. The dishwasher will break down. Maybe it's different for you, but for me, there are so many more needs than there is money.

But we are very blessed. For some, simply being able to pay rent is a huge deal. These parents use food storage or welfare or do whatever it takes to make sure their children are cared for. The thought of a new fence or painting a kitchen seems almost laughable when compared to the harsh reality of much of the world.

Just weeks after the shocking events of September 11, 2001, President Hinckley stood in general conference and said:

> Occasions of this kind pull us up sharply to a realization that life is fragile. . . . We have been counseled again and again concerning self-reliance, concerning debt, concerning thrift. So many of our people are heavily in debt for things that are not entirely necessary. When I was a young man, my

> father counseled me to build a modest home, sufficient for the needs of my family, and make it beautiful and attractive and pleasant and secure. He counseled me to pay off the mortgage as quickly as I could so that, come what may, there would be a roof over the heads of my wife and children. . . . I urge you as members of this Church to get free of debt where possible and to have a little laid aside against a rainy day.[3]

It's a personal struggle for me to put off something I really want. But in a volatile economy where anything can happen, I think I'll trade a perfect house for a feeling of peace. I'd rather know that my family is secure, that we have a little money "laid aside against a rainy day," and live with the wall stains and unfenced backyard a little longer. I'd rather have credit cards paid off, car loans wiped out, and my boys' mission funds started. I'd rather have two marshmallows than one. All it takes is a bit of patience, a bit of faith, and perhaps covering my eyes for a little while. But in the end, I think it will be worth it.

And if I'm lucky, maybe the fence will go up before the grandchildren come along.

Notes

1. Joseph B. Wirthlin, *Finding Peace in Our Lives* (Salt Lake City: Deseret Book, 1995), 16.
2. Shoda, Mischel, and Peake, "Predicting Adolescent Cognitive and Self-Regulatory Competencies from Preschool Delay of Gratification: Identifying Diagnostic Conditions" *Developmental Psychology*, 26 (6:978-986).
3. Gordon B. Hinckley, "The Times in Which We Live," *Ensign*, November 2001, 73.

27

Body Image vs. God's Image

We've become obsessed with beauty and the fountain of youth. . . . I'm really saddened by the way women mutilate their faces in search of that. I see women . . . pulling this up and tucking that back. It's like a slippery slope. . . . It's really insane . . . what society is doing to women."

—Halle Barry [1]

HAVE YOU EVER STOOD IN A STORE LINE ONLY TO CATCH A glimpse of a bikini-clad movie star on a magazine cover? An even tougher question is, did you shake your head in disgust, or did you wish your own stomach was a little flatter? Unfortunately, comparing is something that most women can't help doing. That's why there are so many diet magazines and department store commercials. We all have a desire to be thinner, taller, darker, blonder, or whatever we aren't at the moment. It's a part of human nature.

Women of the World

Now for another question: Who are we, exactly? We have so many places to turn for answers. The magazines at the store reflect the world's view of who we are as women. In fact, they basically scream that we are our bodies. They imply that young, single, beautiful women lead glamorous lives, full of fame and fortune. They also imply that typical moms like me are dull and old-fashioned.

Women's roles seem so cut and dry when we talk about them in church. But when we are pelted with the world's version on TV, billboards, and magazines throughout the week, such beliefs start to sink into even the most determined consciousness. It's almost impossible to avoid these messages. Yet we are reminded that we, as Latter-day Saint mothers, were never meant to chase the whims of the world. A well-known quote from President Kimball explains it well:

> Much of the major growth that is coming to the Church in the last days will come because many of the good women of the world . . . will be drawn to the Church in large numbers. This will happen to the degree that the women of the Church reflect righteousness and articulateness in their lives and to the degree that *the women of the Church are seen as distinct and different—in happy ways—from the women of the world.* Among the real heroines in the world who will come into the Church are women who are more concerned with being righteous than being selfish. These real heroines have true humility, which places a higher value on integrity than on visibility.[2]

We are meant to be different, and that's okay. Our focus as mothers doesn't change—it's society's version of how a woman should look that is constantly shifting. When you take a step back from it all and really watch those ideals change across time, it can be an eye-opening experience.

As an avid art and history fan, I enjoyed a recent trip to Italy. But even my studies of art didn't prepare me for the constant barrage of sculptures depicting unclothed women. Although my husband was uncomfortable, I couldn't help but laugh. These women, considered the "ideal" in centuries past, would be a bit chubby by today's model standards. And yet, such honesty in art was a strange relief. It made me feel a lot better about my body!

These ideals change across history, but also across modern culture. The controversial Padaung women, sometimes called the "giraffe ladies," wear neck rings throughout their life to stretch their necks. This swan-like look is considered beautiful in their culture. The neck-stretching starts with a single ring at age six, then ends at as many as twenty rings by advanced adulthood. [3] Many in Western civilization think the result looks rather strange, but I'm sure the Padaung would consider a lot of our ideals unnatural as well.

Remember the story of the star-bellied Sneetches in Dr. Suess's classic tale? A Sneetch's entire worth was wrapped up in whether he had a star on his belly or not. The solution of applying a star to his belly for equality only ended up in confusion as to the social standing of each Sneetch. It wasn't until the Sneetches stopped caring about belly pictures and focused on each other that they found happiness. [4]

The star versus non-star approach seems rather ridiculous to us, but that's the whole point. The world's ideal is always changing. Fashions come and go, hairstyles change by the year, and we sometimes throw our money at things that don't last past the season. Even more tragic, though, is basing our actual worth on such frivolity.

We were never meant to be a part of all that. We need to look our best, and we need to be healthy, but our worth is not wrapped up in our bodies. Our bodies—old or young, fat or thin, tall or short—are not us. Our bodies are sacred and should be treated as such, but our bodies are only a part of who we are inside. As my time in Romania taught me, a small or shriveled body can house a huge spirit.

Elder Jeffrey R. Holland said: "I plead with you [women] to please be more accepting of yourselves, including your body shape and style, with a little less longing to look like someone else. We are all different. Some are tall, and some are short. Some are round, and some are thin. And almost everyone at some time or other wants to be something they are not!"[5]

> Our bodies—old or young, fat or thin, tall or short—are not us. Our bodies are sacred and should be treated as such, but our bodies are only a part of who we are inside.

Why is it so hard to rise above such things? How does the world's idea of beauty get so ingrained? My husband can wander around town in his basketball shorts, socks and sandals, and disheveled hair with no problem (and he frequently does, to my dismay). And yet, when I drop off my daughter at school, I feel a need to wear dark sunglasses and a hat to cover my bare face and greasy hair. The very thought of going all day without makeup makes me cringe.

The saddest part of all is that I sometimes base my self-worth on a little number displayed on the tag of my pants. Being fit and healthy is important, of course. But for me, that number has too much power in my sense of identity. I tell myself daily that if it would go down a digit or two, suddenly I'd feel a lot better about who I am. Then I could be happy.

Women of God

Who are we, really?

Sheri L. Dew told the story of a forty-five-year-old mother with six children who figured that out. The woman reported that when she had stopped immersing herself in magazines that flooded her mind with pictures of how her home and wardrobe should look, she had started to feel more at peace. She said, "I may be chubby, gray, and wrinkled, but I am a chubby, gray, wrinkled daughter of God, who knows me and loves me."[6]

It's interesting that the magazines were robbing her of peace. As soon as she stopped the endless comparing, she began to see her eternal worth rather than her temporal worth.

Did you know that the scriptures tell us how we should look? I'm not referring to the dress standards in the *For the Strength of Youth* pamphlet, but rather an eternal and fundamental type of appearance. All of the exalted beings will have it. It is one of the most important requirements in the Lord's kingdom, and it is mentioned several times:

- "Can you look up, having the image of God engraven upon your countenances?" (Alma 5:19)
- "Their countenances shone, and the radiance from the presence of the Lord rested upon them (Doctrine and Covenants 138:23–24).
- "Blessed is the people that know the joyful sound: they shall walk, O Lord, in the light of thy countenance" (Psalm 89:15).

President Faust once described this phenomenon. "A sacred light comes to our eyes and countenances when we have a personal bond with our loving Heavenly Father and His Son, our Savior and Redeemer."[7]

Imagine the change that could occur in the world if we focused more on "God's image" than "body image." We probably won't ever be able to change society's view of the perfect woman, but we *can* change our own perspectives.

It is sobering to think that my sweet daughter will soon be tossed around by the same winds of uncertainty and body image that I was. I hope she gains a testimony of who she truly is before the world's shallow beliefs get to her. But I know that the first step begins with me as her mother. I want her to see me without makeup on occasion. I want her to feel that sweatpants are okay sometimes, that a ponytail is not a failure, and that my worth is not based on the tag in my jeans. I want her to look past the magazines at the checkout stand. Most of all, I want her to know that she is unconditionally loved.

I suspect that our Heavenly Father feels the same way about you and me. Let us live with our heads held high, for we are daughters of God, and our bodies do not define us.

Notes

1. Halle Barry, quoted in "Halle Slams 'Insane' Plastic Surgery," *This Is London*, August 2, 2004, www.thisislondon.com/showbiz/articles/12312096?source=PA.
2. Spencer W. Kimball, "The Role of Righteous Women," *Ensign,* November 1979, 103–4, emphasis added.
3. Bjorn Schiermer, *Fashion Theory* 14, Issue 1, 2010, 90.
4. Dr. Suess, *The Sneeches and Other Stories* (New York: Random House, 1961) 3–22.
5. Jeffrey R. Holland, "To Young Women," *Ensign,* November 2005, 29.
6. Anonymous, as quoted by Sheri L. Dew, "We Are Women of God," *Ensign*, November 1999, 98.
7. James E. Faust, "The Light in Their Eyes," *Ensign*, November 2005, 22.

28

Be the Change

"Arise and shine forth, that thy light may be a standard for the nations."

—Doctrine and Covenants 115:5

IT WAS A TYPICAL DAY AT THE MANTI PAGEANT. HEAVY CROWDS made their way slowly to the show. Protesters stood squarely with their signs, watching as the pageant-goers avoided eye contact and stepped carefully around them.

But then something happened. One of the shuffling crowd noticed something different about one of the protestors. Standing in the crowd was a clean cut young man with a large sign and a smile. As the group shuffled slowly along, the observer started to chuckle, then full-out laugh. His friends looked closely at the young man's sign and began to point it out to others. It was then that the protestors actually noticed that the boy wasn't their own. His sign read, "God loves Mormons, and so do I." That clean-cut young man, Andrew, is now faithfully serving a mission.

Not everyone has the mind to take a stand like that. It's much easier to stay back and watch. A popular song by John Mayer states that we are "waiting on the world to change." While that approach may evoke tender longing for a better situation, it doesn't really call us to action.

As predicted by prophets, the world is in turmoil and will not spontaneously change itself. In fact, things will probably get much worse before they get better. As the adversary gains power, we are also asked to increase our spiritual preparation.

Sheri Dew said that "We no longer have the luxury of spending our energy on anything that does not lead us and our families to Christ. . . . In the days ahead, a casual commitment to Christ will not carry us through."[1]

We all know which side will win the battle of souls. Yet we'd sometimes "like to live in that eternal city and still keep a 'summer home' in Babylon."[2] It isn't comfortable to take a stand, that's for sure. We don't want to risk offending people, and we certainly don't want to ruin relationships. But some things are more important than that. Some things we just can't leave alone. Even Andrew needed courage as he braved the protesters. In fact, it seems that the teenagers of the world—who truly believe that they can be astronauts and CEOs and change the world if they darn well please—are an example to us all.

While in high school, my younger sister was shocked by a poster in the window of a certain lingerie store in the mall. Rather than glancing away and passing by as most of us would, she went home and called the manager. (Talk about a teenager with guts!) The manager thanked her for the feedback and promptly took down the poster.

A fourteen-year-old girl from Maine made national news recently when she petitioned the publisher of a popular teen magazine to stop airbrushing photos of their teenage models.[3]

If teenagers can do it, we can do it. Our Young Women are taught to "Stand for truth and righteousness," and each Sunday they pledge to "stand as witnesses of God at all times, and in all things, and in all places."[4] Shouldn't we stand with them?

We should never allow the world to desensitize us so well that we overlook a chance to make the world a little better. They say that it's better to aim for the stars and miss than to aim for a pile of manure and hit it. Even when we do shoot for the stars—writing letters and emails to companies, protesting and signing petitions, and getting involved—we may not accomplish anything more than using up postage stamps. But what an example we are setting for our children. We are sending the message that "This is not okay, and I'm trying to do something about it." We are showing our kids that one person can make a difference. And frequently, that's exactly what happens.

A favorite poem by Edward Everett Hale says:

> I am only one
> But still I am one.
> I cannot do everything,
> But still I can do something;
> And because I cannot do everything
> I will not refuse to do the something that
> I can do.[5]

In elementary school, a friend came up to me at recess. "Are you a Mormon?" she asked cautiously. A twinge of fear fluttered in my young stomach. If I said yes, would she stop being my friend? I swallowed hard and said, "Yes," but then followed it with, "I don't know why people think that's so weird. Mormons are regular people too."

Her next question froze on her lips, and her face fell. Then she said, "Okay. . . . Thanks," and walked away.

I've changed the ending to that story a dozen times in my mind. I want to scream at my young self, "Ask her what she wants to know about Mormons, or bear your testimony, or ask what she knows about our Church. Say *anything*." That opportunity to share what I believe, lost forever, will always haunt me. I have since responded to every opportunity to share my beliefs. So far I have been surprised by how often those opportunities present themselves

The Savior counseled, "Let your light so shine before men, that they may see your good works, and glorify your Father which is in heaven" (Matthew 5:16).

Our "lights" may seem dim at first. But if enough of us put our tiny lights together, we will create a flame bright enough to become a beacon. There is a gentle peace in trying to make society a better place because we were here. Whether in small ways or big ones, let's all go make a difference. It will help us individually and as families, and if we're lucky, it'll make the world a little better too.

Notes

1. Sheri L. Dew, "We Are Women of God," *Ensign*, Nov. 1999, 98.
2. Sharon G. Larsen, "Agency—A Blessing and a Burden," *Ensign*, Nov. 1999, 12; The phrase "summer home in Babylon" probably originated with Neal A. Maxwell, *A Wonderful Flood of Light*, BYU devotional, March 26, 1989.
3. Stephanie Grimes, KSL.com, General News, Salt Lake City, UT. http://www.ksl.com/?nid=1010&sid=20262046
4. Young Women Theme, *Personal Progress*. Published by the Church of Jesus Christ of Latter-day Saints.
5. Edward Everett Hale, *Masterpieces of Religious Verse*, ed. James Dalton Morrison (New York: Harper & Bros., 1948) 416.

29

An Understanding Heart

"Don't judge me because I sin differently than you."

—President Dieter F. Uchtdorf,
quoting a bumper sticker [1]

DESPERATE TO GET MY CHILDREN OUT OF THE HOUSE ON A winter day, I took them to a certain colorful fast food restaurant with a play-place for lunch. As we crossed the parking lot, a child on either side of me and a baby in my arms, a group of teenagers were standing by the door. One was smoking a cigarette. All were dressed in black and had *very* interesting hair. I instinctively drew my children closer to me and tried to glance around discreetly for another entrance. Just then, one of the teens saw me and stepped quickly to the door, pulling it open. I'm sure I blushed as I muttered my thanks, and he smiled widely and said, "Have a great day!"

Guilt. Thinking back, I realize that as a child in southern California, I probably wouldn't have given the group a second look. But as a mother, suddenly my protective instincts kicked in, and I'd had to make a decision—was it safe for my precious little family?

The judging itself isn't necessarily bad. In fact, we should make judgments. The Savior counseled us to "Judge not unrighteously, that ye be not judged, but judge righteous judgment" (Matthew 7:1, JST). He didn't say, "Don't judge anyone, ever." Of course we need to avoid unsafe situations. But the key is to make righteous judgments.

To children, judging someone is pretty black and white. They're either a good guy or a bad guy. End of story. As adults, we are required to look a little deeper. 1 Samuel 16:7 says, "The Lord seeth not as a man seeth; for man looketh on the outward appearance, but the Lord looketh on the heart."

The Gift of Understanding

My daughter frequently insists that she is the "Queen of the World." Since she dominates her two younger brothers, her declaration is at least partly true. I often wonder what the world would be like if she truly were the queen. There would surely be much more chocolate ice cream, twirly skirts, and glitter pens. But like most of us, she wouldn't know the first thing about running a country.

King Solomon, conversely, was a truly humble king who wanted to become a great ruler. Rather than focusing on himself and his own wants, he asked God for a special gift. "Give therefore thy servant an understanding heart to judge thy people, that I may discern between good and bad" (1 Kings 3:9). Of all things, he requested an understanding heart. Isn't that interesting?

His profession was to be a judge over his people, so he wanted to do the best he could. In modern times it isn't our job to judge (usually), yet we crank out judgments all day long. It's easy to do. Our brains automatically categorize everyone we see into neat little mental bins—that is, everyone but ourselves. President Spencer W. Kimball emphasized the quote, "we spend too much time confessing other people's sins."[2] Perhaps with the gift of an understanding heart, the bins would disappear as we learned to see each other's hearts more clearly.

One of the most poignant examples of an understanding heart is the story of the woman taken in adultery in John 8. She was guilty. There was no doubt of that. And the punishment was laid out very clearly—she was to be stoned.

The Savior did two significant things here. First, He distinguished the sin from the sinner. He showed her unconditional love while still condemning the sin. He forgave her tenderly, then admonished her to "Go, and sin no more" (John 8:3–11).

But He also declared whose right it was to judge. "He that is without sin among you, let him first cast a stone at her" (verse 7). He was the only one without sin. Therefore, He was the only one there with the right to judge her.

Had He been absent, the law would have taken effect, and she would have been punished. But the Savior's law transcends our laws. He has bought us with a price (1 Corinthians 6:20). We are His. So when we are told that "I, the Lord, will forgive whom I will forgive, but of you it is required to forgive all men" (Doctrine and Covenants 64:10), it is His right as the one who took all of our sins upon Himself. Therefore we are commanded to leave the "good guy–bad guy" judgments to the Lord. Unfortunately, that is sometimes really, *really* hard to do.

In a strange way, though, isn't it kind of liberating? I don't think I would want that kind of responsibility.

The Judge

My father is an attorney. When he first began practicing law, he was given the criminal defense cases (basically the ones no one else wanted). He suspected that most of his clients were guilty, and so did everyone else, but they were still entitled to a fair trial. My dad had to swallow his feelings and defend each rapist, murderer, thief, or drunk driver to the best of his ability.

One day, he had to meet with a client at the city jail. I was running errands with him that day. When we pulled up, he told me to stay in the car. Knowing this wouldn't be a short meeting, I groaned and said, "Why are you so paranoid? If you don't think he's innocent, why represent him?"

He gave me a long look before replying, "Innocence is the judge's call, not mine. He looks at the evidence on both sides and makes a determination. I just make sure my client's side gets considered equally."

I wouldn't want to be a judge, that's for sure. A judge must stay above the evidence, looking closely at testimony and evidence to decide the fate of a person. I couldn't handle the weight of such a decision. It's so much easier to have faith in the justice system when you're not a part of it. Just deciding which of my kids to punish during an argument makes me want to throw my hands up in despair!

What a relief, then, to know that the responsibility of final judgment rests on the shoulders of another (especially an all-knowing Other). Our responsibility as fellow brothers and sisters is not to condemn, but to try to have an understanding heart.

However, we still have to judge to a point. My father wasn't naïve enough to allow me to visit his client with him. That would have been careless. Perhaps my fear of the door-opening teenager was unfounded, but I will continue to be cautious with strangers.

What a relief to know that the responsibility of final judgment rests on the shoulders of another (especially an all-knowing Other). Our responsibility as fellow brothers and sisters is not to condemn, but to try to have an understanding heart.

We also have a no-sleepover policy with our kids. It may be a bit far-fetched, but it will prevent issues from developing in our children's teen years. We are also very careful about who babysits our precious little ones, and we review safety precautions with them often. Parents have to be more cautious than ever these days.

When it comes to finding the line between the safety of our kids and righteous judgments, perhaps we simply need to follow the Spirit. We need to have the Holy Ghost be such a part of our lives that we just know when it is time to use another exit, or stay in the car, or even keep a child home from a party. Mothers have a keen sense of such things, and we should definitely listen to that voice.

It's blasted hard to leave the verdict to the Lord sometimes, especially when our harsh judgments appear quite justified. But we don't know the experiences that shape and define a perpetrator. We can't read minds or see into the past of a person. Each of us is a sinner to some degree, just as each is a child of God. As President Uchtdorf quoted in the introduction to this chapter, we simply sin differently.

In the words of Henry Wadsworth Longfellow, "Being all fashioned of the self-same dust/ Let us be merciful as well as just."[3]

Notes

1. Dieter F. Uchtdorf, "The Merciful Obtain Mercy," *Ensign*, April 2012, 71.
2. Anonymous, quoted by Spencer W. Kimball, *Miracle of Forgiveness* (Salt Lake City: Bookcraft, 1969), 31.
3. Henry Wadsworth Longfellow, *The Complete Poetical Works of Henry.*

30

The Most Ignored Commandment

"Resolve to be tender with the young, compassionate with the aged, sympathetic with the striving, and tolerant of the weak and the wrong. Sometime in life you will have been all of these."

—Dr. Robert H. Goddard[1]

THERE'S A UNIVERSAL LAW IN EFFECT HERE ON EARTH. THAT law is the same throughout cultures, religions, and communities. The law is simple, yet profound enough to change nations as well as the weakest heart.

There are several versions: "What goes around, comes around." "Treat others as you want to be treated." Some call it *karma*, or the "boomerang effect." General Authorities call it the "Law of the Harvest." Whichever term you prefer, the Golden Rule is just as valid in the home as it is on the freeway. What a scary thought.

The Savior said it well: "Therefore all things whatsoever ye would that men should do to you, do ye even so to them; for this is the law and the prophets" (Matthew 7:12). President Hinckley called it the "most commonly known and probably the least commonly observed" of all the commandments. [2]

Why do you think he called it that? There are a lot of broken commandments out there. Watch TV for just ten minutes and you'll see people treading all over the "Thou shalt not commit adultery" and "Thou shalt not kill" commandments, just to name a couple. But I suppose one reason he said that is because the Golden Rule seems to transcend most other parts of the Law of Moses. If we truly treat others the way we want to be treated, we will also honor our parents, avoid stealing, and obey the law. We will just be better people.

The Savior was the ultimate example of this law. He healed the sick, raised the dead, and took upon Himself the sins of countless souls. Surely He has a right to ask that we treat each other with kindness as well.

We never know how far-reaching our little acts of service may become. Here is a story that touches my heart, because the woman mentioned could easily have been myself. A severe storm caused heavy delays and flight cancellations at busy Chicago O'Hare International Airport. Thousands of frustrated people were stranded. Among those in trouble was a young pregnant mother with a wailing two-year-old at her feet. She was sick and exhausted. Her doctor had warned her to avoid bending or picking up anything heavy, so as the line moved she pushed her tired and crying child forward with her foot. People made critical remarks at this, but no one offered to assist her. Then a smiling man approached, saying, "You need help. Let me help you." He picked up the dirty child and offered her a piece of gum, holding her gently as she calmed down.

He didn't stop there. He spoke with the others in line to explain her need and then took her to the front of the line, helping her get checked in. Then he found her a seat, chatted for a moment, and left without giving his name.

Years later a letter arrived at Church Headquarters. It said:

> Dear President Kimball:
>
> I am a student at Brigham Young University. I have just returned from my mission in Munich, West Germany. I had a lovely mission and learned much. . . . I was sitting in priesthood meeting last week, when a story was told of a loving service which you performed some twenty-one years ago in the Chicago airport. The story told of how you met a young pregnant mother with a . . . screaming child, in . . . distress, waiting in a long line for her tickets. She was threatening miscarriage and therefore couldn't lift her child to comfort her. She had experienced four previous miscarriages, which gave added reason for the doctor's orders not to bend or lift. You comforted the crying child and explained the dilemma to the other passengers in line. This act of love took the strain and tension off my mother. I was born a few months later in Flint, Michigan. I just want to *thank you* for your love. *Thank you* for your example![3]

The effects of service aren't always this remarkable, but little acts of kindness can ripple across many lives and even generations. As mothers, we especially have the opportunity of influence. We speak kindly to our children so they will learn to speak kindly back. We serve faithfully in the church just as we are served faithfully. We cherish our spouses with all our hearts in the hopes that it will be returned. We compliment and lift and encourage. We listen with an open heart and open arms. Mothers are naturally better suited for the Golden Rule than anyone else.

Unfortunately, though, even our less diligent actions can boomerang back to us. I remember my own mother, irritated with something I had done wrong, exclaiming, "I hope you have a child just like you!" Luckily, my children are much better than I was, but I may still have to use that line on my own kids someday.

The more positive vibes we deliver to society, the more that are likely to come back to us. But even if they don't come back, we will be that much more like our Savior. And that doesn't sound like such a bad thing either.

Notes

1. Dr. Robert H. Goddard, quoted in *Chicken Soup for the Soul: Stories for a Better World* (New York: Scholastic, 2005), 88.
2. Gordon B. Hinckley, "Do Ye Even So To Them," *Ensign*, December 1991, 2–3.
3. Ibid, 4.

31

The Gift of Forgiveness

"I am calm as a summer's morning; I have a conscience void of offense towards God, and towards all men."

—Joseph Smith, Doctrine and Covenants 135:4

As a young girl, I had a brilliant idea. I would start writing down my sins. That way I could remember them when I knelt down to pray at night, and I could "repent." Made sense, right? So for several nights I went down the checklist as I prayed. "Sorry for calling my sister an alien," "Sorry for telling my mom that I don't do chores anymore," and "Forgive me for thinking that Sister So-and-so had flabby arms." (That one would definitely come back around later.) After a while, my checklist began to look the same. Every night I was "repenting" of the same things.

It was a noble effort, especially for a nine-year-old. But I didn't quite understand the concepts of repentance and forgiveness. I didn't understand the two most important aspects of the Atonement: why it was necessary and how to truly apply it in my life.

Why the Atonement

I won't pretend to completely fathom the Atonement, but I have seen its effects. I have, thankfully, learned the proper way to repent. However, the hardest part of repentance can be the "forgive and forget" part. It can be really hard for me to forgive others who have committed wrongs, especially when they don't seem to be sorry at all. And it's *really* hard to forgive myself when I'm at fault. It's difficult to place my burden on the Savior's shoulders without keeping a portion of it as a trophy or a beating stick.

President Spencer W. Kimball said: "The essence of the miracle of forgiveness is that *it brings peace* to the previously anxious, restless, frustrated, perhaps tormented soul. In a world of turmoil and contention, this is indeed a priceless gift." [1]

We all have the same access to the Atonement. It doesn't matter who we're related to or how much money we have, how many quilts we've tied for charity, or how many times we've been arrested. The Savior has atoned for anyone who will accept His offering.

Some would say that such equality is unfair. The prodigal son's righteous older brother thought that too. [2]

So did some of the laborers in the vineyard in Matthew 20. The householder hired some laborers for a penny. While they worked, he continued to send more men throughout the afternoon. For the last hour, he hired a final group. When the day's work was done, everyone was paid a penny. The morning workers grumbled, "These last hath wrought but one hour, and thou hast made them equal unto us, which have borne the burden and heat of the day" (Matthew 20:1–12).

Elder Jeffrey R. Holland said of this parable:

> It is with that reading of the story that I feel the grumbling of the first laborers must be seen. As the householder in the parable tells them (and I paraphrase only slightly): "My friends, I am not being unfair to you. You agreed on the wage for the day, a good wage. You were very happy to get the work, and I am very happy with the way you served. You are paid in full. Take your pay and enjoy the blessing. As for the others,

surely I am free to do what I like with my own money." Then this piercing question to anyone then or now who needs to hear it: *"Why should you be jealous because I choose to be kind?"* [3]

God will forgive whom He chooses, but we are required to forgive everyone (Doctrine and Covenants 64:10). This also includes ourselves. Whether the offender knows or cares that we have forgiven them doesn't matter. What matters is that we are at peace with ourselves and with others. We have given our burden away and refuse to carry it any more. We have more joyful burdens to carry, like raising our children.

How to Use the Atonement

Elder H. Burke Peterson told the story of a group of teens at a desert picnic in central Arizona. Suddenly one girl was bitten on the ankle by a rattlesnake. They knew they should seek medical help to remove the venom from her leg, but first the girl and her friends chose to find the snake and seek their revenge. It took fifteen or twenty minutes. Finally they found it and avenged the injury with rocks and stones. By now the girl was suffering from the effects of the venom, and her friends rushed her to the emergency room.

Two days later, Elder Peterson was asked by some of the girl's friends to visit her in the hospital. He said: "As I entered her room, I saw a pathetic sight. Her foot and leg were elevated—swollen almost beyond recognition. The tissue in her limb had been destroyed by the poison, and a few days later it was found her leg would have to be amputated below the knee." [4]

What a tragic and senseless end. Most of us read that story and think, "Everyone knows you go to the hospital, not look for the snake." And yet, how often do we seek out our own personal reptiles? How often do we take hold of the poison of bitterness and let it fester, refusing to release the pain?

It is said that "women and elephants never forget an injury."[5] That statement may be a bit unfair, but my husband certainly agrees with it. My mind is certainly too organization-oriented for its own good. When my husband does things that are hurtful (which, admittedly, happens rarely) my brain files his actions into a bin in my mind. Each time he unknowingly repeats the action, the bin gets heavier and more organized. Soon I have an imaginary argument all set up—complete with examples, quotes, and a thesis statement. It takes genuine, purposeful, eye-popping effort to lift that bin over my head and dump it into the mental recycling bin.

Yet that is what we are asked to do. If we want peace, we have to forgive. Picking at the scabs of a careless word or action on someone else's part only prolongs the healing process. Refusing to forgive someone only hurts ourselves. We all know this, and yet sometimes it seems impossible to do—the ultimate "easier said than done" proposition.

President Uchtdorf said:

> When we feel hurt, angry, or envious, it is quite easy to judge other people, often assigning dark motives to their actions in order to justify our own feelings of resentment. . . . Of course, we know this is wrong. . . . We all depend on the Savior; none of us can be saved without Him. . . . Forgiveness for our sins comes with conditions. We must repent, and we must be willing to forgive others. Jesus taught, 'Forgive one another; for he that forgiveth not . . . [stands] condemned before the Lord; for there remaineth in him the greater sin.' . . . Of course, these words seem perfectly reasonable—when applied to someone else. . . . We can so clearly and easily see the harmful results that come when *others* judge and hold grudges. But when it comes to our own prejudices and grievances, we too often justify our anger as righteous and our judgment as reliable and only appropriate. [6]

A sister in my ward, a native of Puerto Rico, didn't meet her father until she was an adult. By then she had suffered decades of poverty and resented the man she felt had abandoned her.

Eventually she married, started a family, and began on her family history work. One day she came across some questions that only her father could answer. At that point she had only spoken with her father twice, and neither conversation had convinced her that he was anyone worth having in her life.

But she swallowed her pride, gathered some courage, and made the call. It was a polite conversation at first. As her questions continued, his voice softened as he began to recall his childhood and the ones he loved. There was laughter, there were stories of joy and harmony, and he sounded like—well, like a regular person. The villain in her mind was slipping away. When she finally hung up the phone, she began to cry. Her husband asked what was wrong. She tearfully replied, "I think I love my father."

We can set our household in order, become wonderful mothers, and fulfill all our callings with dedication. But if we can't forgive, we will never have the lasting peace that the Lord offers. If you need help forgiving someone, even if it is yourself, seek the help available to you. In addition to prayer, talking with a concerned bishop, a qualified counseling professional, and even loving Relief Society sisters or friends can be a huge relief. It is worth any price to live knowing that your soul is, as the Prophet Joseph said before his death, "void of offense toward God and toward all men" (Doctrine and Covenants 135:4).

Allow your soul to be at peace.

Notes

1. Spencer W. Kimball, *The Miracle of Forgiveness*, 363, emphasis added.

2. See Luke 15:27–30.
3. Jeffrey R. Holland, "The Laborers in the Vineyard," *Ensign*, May 2012, 31.
4. H. Burke Peterson, "Removing the Poison of an Unforgiving Spirit," *Ensign*, November 1983, 59.
5. Reginald. *Reginald on Besetting Sins* (London: Westminster Gazette, 1911).
6. Dieter F. Uchtdorf, "The Merciful Obtain Mercy," *Ensign*, May 2012, 70.

Puzzle Piece #6

Mother of Joy

A mother of joy looks to her husband as an equal partner and helpmate in their journey together. She understands that her mind is powerful and can influence her mood. She tries to see the positive during even the hardest of trials. A joyful mother treasures the fleeting moments with her children and makes memories with them that will last for generations.

32

Captain and First Officer: The Perfect Team

"[A] bride sighed blissfully on her wedding day, 'Mom, I'm at the end of all my troubles!' 'Yes,' replied her mother, 'but at which end?'"

—Elder Bruce C. Hafen [1]

My brother-in-law is a commercial airline pilot. He once told me that many airplane crashes result from a breakdown in communication between pilots. The airline requires both a captain and a first officer to be present because they cross-check each other. When one makes a mistake, regardless of seniority or experience, the other has the responsibility to catch and correct it. Occasionally a mistake is made, and the other pilot keeps his concerns to himself. That decision creates a dangerous environment that puts the entire flight at risk. But usually, the captain and first officer make a great team; guiding the flight, passengers, and cargo to their destination in safety.

The family unit was designed to be led by two parents for the same reason. The eternal well-being of the family is their goal and ultimate destination. Husbands and wives, regardless of roles and experience, usually work together. Occasionally one will pull more than his or her weight for a while, and sometimes one will make a mistake. But the two usually balance each other out, and together they are more likely to stay on course.

Despite what Hollywood and political columns say, there is a large percentage of fully functional marriages in the United States today. While divorce rates continue to skyrocket at alarming rates, thousands of couples quietly celebrate their fortieth and fiftieth (or more) wedding anniversaries each year. We don't see them on TV, and we don't read about them in magazines or in books very often. But these amazing couples place their marriages squarely in the center of their lives. They work unnoticed in the background to keep their families strong in the midst of ever-increasing cynicism.

My own parents' divorce wasn't entirely unexpected, but it caused such a nuclear blast of anguish for our family that I became absolutely determined to make our marriage divorce-proof. Yet, I didn't want to simply avoid divorce—I wanted to have a happy marriage!

Those happily-married-for-fifty-years couples have much to teach us. They emit such a sense of respect and honor for each other that they seem blissfully happy at any age. Such couples seem to have three major attributes in common: 1) optimism and a sense of humor, 2) commitment, and 3) humility.

Optimism and a Sense of Humor

Most strong couples have these qualities. Often they are inherited from optimistic parents or a happy childhood. But sometimes these attributes don't come easily. They may require a little practice. Our Primary children sing about one of the most effective ways to do just that:

No one likes a frowning face.
Change it for a smile.
Make the world a better place
By smiling all the while.[2]

This song is profound because it reflects a process. First, we realize that our mood is negatively affecting others. Then we force ourselves to emit a more positive outward appearance, which makes our environment better. And the best part is, this fake-it-till-you-make-it attitude can actually lift us for real. When I force myself to slow down and smile more often, it truly does affect my emotions for the better. And that determination to lift my spirits tends to lift my marriage as well.

A wonderful example of a positive—and amusing, I might add—marriage is that of President and Sister Hinckley. It was strong from the very beginning. When they were engaged, young Gordon Hinckley expressed his concern about marrying because he only had $150 in the bank (it was during the Great Depression). With her trademark humor, Marjorie later said, "I had hoped for a husband and now I was getting $150 too!"[3]

With such a heavy calling to bear, surely President Hinckley was grateful he had a wife who could make him laugh. One day, while standing at the pulpit next to his wife at an area conference, President Hinckley tenderly discussed their time together and began to weep. Marjorie leaned forward and said, "Has it been that bad?"[4]

Their philosophy can perhaps be summed up by his words, "In all of living, have much fun and laughter. Life is to be enjoyed, not just endured."[5] They were married sixty-six years before her death, and I would imagine that those years were vibrant and full of joy.

There is something so attractive about a positive attitude. Such optimism, when coupled within a marriage, surely has the ability to overcome even the most difficult trial.

Dr. John Gottman, a researcher, discovered what many call the golden ratio, or the secret to successful relationships. He said that the ratio of positive to negative interaction was 5:1. In other words, for every one negative comment, there needed to be five positive ones for the couple to remain effective.[6] It takes effort, though, to see the positive when our eternal companion throws his clothes on the floor instead of in the hamper sitting two feet away (but I'm not bitter). It takes real commitment to bite back a sarcastic retort or praise our husband to the neighbor when we've had a disagreement that morning. Constructive feedback (disagreements, essentially) can be necessary on occasion. But such interactions should only be one-fifth or less of our conversations. I've known couples who have this system down so well that the ratio is closer to 100:1. Imagine their happiness in such a marriage.

Marriage is intended to be the happiest institution in the world. We are encouraged (or pushed, if you went to BYU) to marry because "men [and women] are that they might have joy" (2 Nephi 2:25), and because "marriage is ordained of God" (Doctrine and Covenants 49:15).

Yet, this happiness in marriage doesn't usually come without effort. It's hard work, and that work begins long before the marriage date. Jenkins Lloyd Jones, as quoted by President Hinckley, wrote:

> There seems to be a superstition among many thousands of our young who hold hands and smooch in the drive-ins that marriage is a cottage surrounded by perpetual hollyhocks to which a perpetually young and handsome husband comes home to a perpetually young and ravishing wife. When the hollyhocks wither and boredom and bills appear the divorce courts are jammed. . . . Anyone who imagines that bliss is normal is going to waste a lot of time running around shouting that he has been robbed.[7]

We all want happy marriages. Knowing how to keep it that way, though, can be the tricky part. Positive and vibrant couples know that their own happiness is entwined with that of their spouse. Happiness isn't simply what's left when trials and troubles are gone, but rather something that takes a conscious decision and determined action.

During one family home evening in our home, the topic was service. After trying unsuccessfully to use scripture references to illustrate the point (at which point our young children were rolling around on the floor and hiding under the table), we decided to implement something a little more hands-on: the "Secret Friend." Each person took a name and promised to do random acts of service for that person all week long. My husband drew my name.

Rather than buying candy or making the bed, as I would have done, he took a few minutes to write down all the things he loved about me. Then he hid each tiny slip of paper where I would find it throughout the next day. I opened the refrigerator and was greeted by a declaration that I was beautiful. I poked my foot into a shoe with a note inside that read, "You make delicious meals. Thank you." (I should have hung that one on the fridge as a reminder for both of us.)

Those notes brightened my week as nothing else could have. I felt appreciated, cherished, and thoroughly loved. That was the beginning of our note-hiding. We still hide notes for each other on occasion. When I go to bed before he gets home, I write him a message on the bathroom mirror (with a dry-erase marker, of course) for him to read while he brushes his teeth. Occasionally we will call each other while he is at work just to connect for a few minutes. He holds my hand in public and still, after eight years, opens the car door for me. I know that my husband loves me, but I also know that he shows me, and that's almost more important.

Bottom line: Optimism and a sense of humor are critical to a married couple, and they lead us to forget about ourselves and serve one another. This is the secret to true happiness in a marriage.

Commitment

We all know that marriages in general are under attack by the adversary, but it's difficult to remember that our own marriages are no exception. Not only does marriage have the potential to make us happy, but it also creates eternal families—the sore spot of the adversary.

Like many young couples, we were so caught up in the excitement of our wedding day that we have forgotten much of the temple sealer's counsel. But as we have returned to the temple for the sealings of others and performed proxy sealings, we are reminded of the covenants we made that day, to each other and to God. Those covenants have a very real power.

> Happiness isn't simply what's left when trials and troubles are gone, but rather something that takes a conscious decision and determined action.

Both of our fathers are attorneys, and my husband works at a law firm, so we are familiar with legal contracts. As you know, a contract is an agreement between two parties. A covenant is an agreement between God and man. All too often we see marriages being treated as contracts instead of covenants—and it's not just in Hollywood. Elder Bruce C. Hafen said:

> When troubles come, the parties to a *contractual* marriage seek happiness by walking away. They marry to obtain benefits and will stay only as long as they're receiving what they bargained for. But when troubles come to a covenant marriage, the husband and wife work them through. They marry to give

> and to grow, bound by covenants to each other, to the community, and to God. *Contract* companions each give 50 percent; *covenant* companions each give 100 percent.[8]

When we focus entirely on the happiness of someone else, we find true joy. This is true in most relationships, but especially in a marriage. Perhaps that is one reason we are encouraged to have families—to make us just a little more like our Savior, whose entire life was dedicated to others.

Elder Hafen continued:

> Marrying and raising children *can* yield the most valuable religious experiences of their lives. Covenant marriage requires a total leap of faith: they must keep their covenants without knowing what risks that may require of them. They must surrender unconditionally, obeying God and sacrificing for each other. Then they will discover what Alma called "incomprehensible joy."[9]

A marriage counselor friend told me that many people think of a new marriage like two lumps of clay—they take two very different sets of traditions, priorities, and personalities and try to mash them together. While this analogy makes sense in some ways, my friend preferred to think of it more like a deck of cards. Each person comes with their own deck, and they have to make a new deck. This means the couple needs to pick and choose the parts that are most important to them and discard the rest. The wife may choose to give up a comfortable tradition such as elaborate or expensive Christmas gifts for the greater good, while her husband may give up Sunday football. But the point is that they are choosing what to implement and discard together—they are choosing the marriage over themselves.

So what is the key, then, to having a covenant marriage?

Elder Russell M. Nelson said, "Harmony in marriage comes only when one esteems the welfare of his or her spouse among the highest of priorities. When that really happens, a celestial marriage becomes a reality, bringing great joy in this life and in the life to come."[10]

As Elder Nelson said, our spouses should remain at the top of the list. Our families will only be as strong as our marriages. That commitment between husband and wife can open the door to a greater happiness and peace of soul than we can imagine. I have seen a glimpse of such joy in my own marriage, and I look forward to many more decades of covenant-keeping bliss.

Humility

Recently, an article by Bryce Peterson in the *Ensign* struck me. He wrote that his parents had a difficult marriage. One of his mother's common complaints was that his father splashed toothpaste on the mirror when he brushed his teeth and never cleaned it up. It began to fester and she couldn't let it go. She ignored her son's comment that in the eternal scheme of things, a little toothpaste on the mirror wasn't a huge deal. Then her husband died. She realized then that she missed him more than she had anticipated. During a visit with his mother months after the funeral, Peterson said:

> Her eyes turned watery as she told me of a mistake that she regretted. She reminded me of the toothpaste and how adamant she had been that he was slothful in neglecting to clean up his mess. She had been so angry over such a small thing. Mom admitted that on the first cleaning day after Dad died, there was toothpaste on the mirror. She cleaned the mirror, but on the second cleaning day, there was more toothpaste on the mirror. The same thing happened on the third and fourth cleaning days as well. Mom realized that she

had blamed Dad for the toothpaste on the mirror for many years, but it had been both of them splashing toothpaste. She felt terrible that for years she had been so upset about such a small thing. She freely admitted that her anger had hurt her much worse than it had affected Dad. [11]

That story is tragic for two reasons: she had allowed something that didn't even matter to get between her and her husband (and it was something she herself also did, no less!), but she had also missed out on the joy that a little more humility could have bestowed on her marriage.

Benjamin Franklin once advised to keep both eyes wide open when choosing a spouse, then one eye closed after.[12] In no other relationship is the counsel of beams and motes in the eye more applicable than in marriage (Matthew 7:1–5). We may notice what our spouses do wrong, yet expect our spouse to take our own annoying habits in stride.

Marriage is the ultimate lesson in patience. The same Book of Mormon chapter that says, "Men are that they might have joy" also contains a verse that declares, "For it must needs be that there is an opposition in all things" (2 Nephi 2:11, 25).

There will be tough times. Men and women are naturally very different. This difference in nature has a purpose. Elder Bednar said:

> By divine design, men and women are intended to progress together toward perfection and a fulness of glory. Because of their distinctive temperaments and capacities, males and females each bring to a marriage relationship unique perspectives and experiences. The man and the woman contribute differently but equally to a oneness and a unity that can be achieved in no other way. The man completes and perfects the woman and the woman completes and perfects the man as they learn from and mutually strengthen and bless

> each other. "Neither is the man without the woman, neither the woman without the man, in the Lord" (1 Corinthians 11:11).[13]

Because we are so different, we have to work together. And because we have to work together, we have to learn to forgive each other. This is perhaps the hardest lesson for me, which probably means it is the most important for me to learn.

The ever-knowing President Hinckley said, "The willingness to forgive is a sign of spiritual and emotional maturity. It is one of the great virtues to which we should all aspire. Imagine a world filled with individuals willing both to apologize and to accept an apology. Is there any problem that could not be solved among people who possessed the humility and largeness of spirit and soul to do either—or both—when needed?"[14]

Temple sealings are eternal when we keep our covenants and stay committed to each other. Yet, it isn't enough to simply raise children together. We need to throw ourselves unequivocally into the happiness of our companions.

Personally, I could do a lot better in this area. Our marriage is quite happy, but there is definite room for improvement. I need to cherish more deeply that special man who chose me for his flight's first officer. I need to do better about overlooking the little things and forgiving the bigger things. I need to focus on changing myself first. I need to have a more positive attitude and inject a little more humor into everyday life. Most of all, I want my marriage to reflect that of Parley P. Pratt. He said:

> It was from [Joseph Smith] that I learned that the wife of my bosom might be secured to me for time and all eternity; and that the refined sympathies and affections which endeared us to each other emanated from the fountain of divine eternal love. . . . I had loved before, but I knew not why. But now

> I loved—with a pureness—an intensity of elevated, exalted feeling, which would lift my soul from the transitory things of this groveling sphere and expand it as the ocean. . . . In short, I could now love with the spirit and with the understanding also. Yet, at that time, my dearly beloved brother, Joseph Smith, had . . . merely lifted a corner of the veil and given me a single glance into eternity.[15]

In the long run, the toothpaste splatters and tossed clothing won't matter. We can't change our spouse. This life is so short that we only have enough time to fix ourselves anyway. Let's remember that our ultimate goal is the same—to get our family to the right destination.

Take your sweetheart's hand, give him a smooch, and enjoy the flight.

Notes

1. Bruce C. Hafen, "Covenant Marriage," *Ensign*, November 1996, 26.
2. "Smiles," *Children's Songbook*, 267.
3. Marjorie Pay Hinckley, *Glimpses Into the Life and Heart of Marjorie Pay Hinckley* (Salt Lake City: Deseret Book, 1999), 77–78.
4. Marjorie Pay Hinckley, quoted by Doug Robinson, *Deseret News*, January 28, 2008. http://www.deseretnews.com/article/695247788/Marjorie-Pay-Hinckley--Every-bit-his-equal.html?pg=all.
5. Gordon B. Hinckley, "Stand True and Faithful," *Ensign*, April 1996.
6. John Gottman, PhD, *Why Marriages Succeed or Fail*, (New York: Simon & Schuster, 1994), 56–57.

7. Jenkins Lloyd Jones, as quoted by Gordon B. Hinckley, "What God Hath Joined Together," *Ensign*, May 1991, 72. See also *Deseret News*, June 12, 1973, A4.
8. Bruce C. Hafen, "Covenant Marriage," Ensign, November 1996, 26.
9. Ibid.
10. Russell M. Nelson, "Celestial Marriage," *Ensign*, November 2008, 94.
11. Bryce Peterson, "Toothpaste on the Mirror," *Ensign*, September 2008, 23.
12. Benjamin Franklin, *Poor Richard's Almanac*. June, as quoted by John Bartlett in *Bartlett's Familiar Quotations* (New York: Little, Brown, & Co., 2002), 319.
13. David A. Bednar, "Marriage is Essential to His Eternal Plan," *Ensign*, June 2006.
14. Gordon B. Hinckley, *Standing for Something* (New York: Random House, 2000), 73.
15. Parley P. Pratt, *Autobiography of Parley P. Pratt*, ed. Parley P. Pratt, Jr. (Salt Lake City: Deseret Book, 1938), 259–60.

33

You Are What You Think

"Each of us, with discipline and effort, has the capacity to control our thoughts and our actions. This is part of the process of developing spiritual, physical, and emotional maturity."

—President Gordon B. Hinckley[1]

I LOVE THE CLASSIC STORY OF ANNE OF GREEN GABLES. IN A sequel, *Anne of the Windy Poplars*, the grown orphan-turned-teacher Anne Shirley has a large capacity for love, a childlike faith in people, and an endlessly positive disposition. She has overcome a rough childhood to become a teacher at Kingsport Ladies College. There she meets her antithesis: Katherine Brooke.

Katherine is the female version of Ebenezer Scrooge. She thinks the worst of everyone and everything. She stifles every bit of light she finds, and she almost succeeds in extinguishing the unconquerable spirit of Anne Shirley. Almost.[2]

We've all met examples of both women in our own lives. While there are extremely positive individuals and extremely dark and negative people, most of us fall somewhere in-between. Hopefully we are more like the Anne Shirleys than the Katherine Brookes of society.

Who Am I?

There was a particularly rough time in my life when I switched from an Anne personality to a Katherine. My mood was unusually overcast. Realizing that something was wrong, I went to see a counselor, who diagnosed me with Seasonal Depression Disorder (also called Seasonal Affective Disorder, or SAD). In other words, the cold and dark winter weather was messing with my emotions. I had two choices: try to deal with it by myself, or treat it with medication. I was reluctant to use medication, but I didn't know how to overcome it on my own, either.

Let me stop here for a disclosure. I'm about to tell you a secret that has helped me with my depression. However, I'm not a doctor, and what worked for me may not work for everyone. Clinical depression is a very real disorder that often requires medication to correct. But as I share with you what I learned while struggling with my own problem, remember that this gospel-based premise can benefit anyone, whether they are suffering from depression or not.

Back to the story. I chose to do more research before going the medication route. So I scoured through conference talks, psychology books, and the scriptures. One day I had a *duh!* moment.

The epiphany? Our thoughts can influence our moods.

You may be saying, "Yeah, that is a no-brainer. Everyone knows that." But think about it. Our thoughts are the precursor of our actions. That is why we are counseled so strongly to control our thoughts. When we control our thoughts, we control everything else about ourselves. Changing our thoughts can actually change our actions and emotions.

The Power of Thought

This idea isn't new. President David O. McKay said, "Every

action is preceded by a thought. If we want to control our actions, we must control our thinking."[3]

I enjoyed my psychology classes in school because they were so fascinating. Some scientists claim that controlling thought has the power to actually change the makeup of a brain. Neuroplasticity is a science that studies the brain's neural pathways and how they can change. In theory, people who are generally positive have deeper positive neural pathways in their minds. People who are generally negative have a well-worn network of negative thought "trenches." But when they force themselves to correct their thinking, their brains will actually form new neural pathways to adapt. It can be really hard, and some people may require medication to make the leap, but many of us can train ourselves to do it. Reprogramming our minds—literally—really is possible. Isn't the human brain incredible?

The point is that, at least to some degree, attitude may be under our control. If we can learn to control our thoughts, we can ultimately control much of our emotions. Positive begets positive, negative begets negative. We reap what we sow (Galatians 6:7).

Benjamin Franklin said, "The foundation of all happiness is thinking rightly."[4]

The concept may feel a bit fluffy at first. Can positive thinking really change all that much? Is it really that simple?

Well, yes and no. It can be a simple concept, but it's definitely not easy. However, I believe that our Father in Heaven wants us to be happy in this life as well as the next. I also believe that He has given us a powerful mind that is capable of much more than we understand. And I believe that we aren't here to be miserable, but to have joy—a joy that isn't the result of ignorant bliss and a lack of real problems in life, but a joy that is constant despite what goes on outside of ourselves.

It Gets Easier with Time

President Heber J. Grant often said, "That which we persist in doing becomes easier for us to do; not that the nature of the thing itself is changed, but that our power to do is increased."[5]

Admittedly, I still struggle with training my mind sometimes. It's been eleven years since my diagnosis, and the wrestle continues. My mood is as dependable as a small-town carnival roller coaster. On sunny days, nothing can get me down. I'm a giddy, confident Anne Shirley. When the weather is cloudy and dark, I prepare myself for more mind training.

But it *is* getting easier. Now I recognize that the issue is outside of myself. (Well, it is inside my mind, but you know what I mean.) When the disorder shoots me continuous thoughts of failure and worthlessness, I mentally catch those negative messages and throw them back like a boomerang, or flip them to the positive in my mind. When I find myself saying things like, "We have such a big yard to mow each week," I flip it in my mind and follow it with, "Isn't it great that we have a yard for the kids to play in?" There's plenty of negative out there, and it slips in unexpectedly. But we do have control over how much power we give to our thoughts. I know that those dark "Katherine" thoughts aren't mine, so I refuse to let them stay.

The World Complies

Just as "we are what we eat," we also are what we think. Proverbs 23:7 says, "For as he thinketh in his heart, so is he." But the world also tends to comply with what we expect. If we think our children are spoiled and selfish, we will probably treat them that way, and they will likely fulfill those expectations. If we feel self-conscious around other women and believe that they don't like us, it will be reflected in our actions, and after a while it will come true.

Bottom line: Negativity only brings negativity. But choosing to see the positive when our mind instantly lists the negatives can actually train our minds to see the good, creating new neural pathways in our brains. When our minds are trained to see the good, we feel better about ourselves and about life. Our thoughts are powerful. They can control our emotions—hopefully for the better.

Change the Focus

In addition to the positive-thinking route, there is another way to experience that peace of mind. It is found in training ourselves to think about others first.

King Benjamin counseled us to "consider on the happy and blessed state of those that keep the commandments of God" (Mosiah 2:41). Living the gospel can make us happy. And the happiest people I know are those who forget themselves.

Elder Marion D. Hanks once told BYU students his secret for helping depression: "At the moment of depression, if you will follow a simple program, you will get out of it. Get on your knees and get the help of God; then get up and go find somebody who needs something that you can help them find. Then it will be a good day."[6]

The Anne Shirleys of the world aren't takers—they are givers. They choose to focus on the needs of others. Somehow, when immersing ourselves into the lives of suffering people, our own problems can melt away. It's hard to be self-absorbed and truly serve someone at the same time.

Luckily, my childhood wasn't anything close to Anne's. I had a wonderful family with a stable home. But we did move quite a bit. I have lived in twenty different wards in my lifetime. While moving to a new place was exciting, I always dreaded that first Sunday at church when I would be a stranger. Some wards were incredibly welcoming and I felt instantly accepted. Others were mediocre in their greeting. It would have been easy to use the members' seeming indifference as an excuse to stay home. But my testimony kept me returning each week, despite my grumbling.

If I had been a bit more mature, I would have done what Mark Skousen, a friend of Elder Oaks, did in a similar situation:

> Years ago, I changed my attitude about going to church. No longer do I go to church for my sake, but to think of others. I make a point of saying hello to people who sit alone, to welcome visitors, . . . to volunteer for an assignment. . . .In short, I go to church each week with the intent of being active, not passive, and making a positive difference in people's lives. Consequently, my attendance at Church meetings is so much more enjoyable and fulfilling. [7]

He used both methods. Not only did he switch to the positive, but he also focused on others first. These methods have a real power for happiness. Elder Oaks, referring to this story, said, "All of this illustrates the eternal principle that we are *happier* and *more fulfilled* when we act and serve for what we give, not for what we get." [8]

Mental Attitude and Trials

Happiness is a major benefit of both service and a positive mindset. But there is another benefit as well. In King Benjamin's speech, he doesn't say, "If you do what is right, you won't have trials Then you can finally be happy." We can think happy thoughts and serve others until we collapse, but trials will still come along. The benefit is that we have more power to overcome the crippling darkness that accompanies such tests of our faith.

This book won't change your mind. Even the most decorated brain surgeon or psychologist can't change your mind. No one has the power to change the way that you think except for you. We have limitless potential when we choose to focus on the positive. Just as Anne Shirley eventually won over the impenetrable Katherine, we can actually make ourselves happier by changing our thoughts and living for others instead of ourselves. Our lives can change, our homes can change, and our relationships with those we love can change—all with the power of the mind.

Notes

1. Gordon B. Hinckley, "Reverence and Morality," *Ensign*, May 1987, 47.
2. L .M. Montgomery, *Anne of the Windy Poplars* (New York: Bantam Books, 1981).
3. David O. McKay, as quoted by Thomas S. Monson, "Preparation Brings Blessings," *Ensign*, May 2010, 66.
4. Benjamin Franklin, *Benjamin Franklin's The Art of Virtue*, ed. George L. Rogers (Eden Prairie: Acorn Publishing, 1996), 89.
5. Heber J. Grant, *Conference Report*, April 1901, 63.
6. Marion D. Hanks, "Make it a Good Day!" *BYU Speeches of the Year 1966–67* (Provo, UT: Brigham Young University Press, 1967), 7. As quoted by John Bytheway, *When Times are Tough.*
7. Mark Skousen, as quoted by Dallin H. Oaks, "Unselfish Service," *Ensign*, April 2009, 96.
8. Dallin H. Oaks, "Unselfish Service," *Ensign*, April 2009, 96.

Puzzle Piece #7

Mother of Peace

A MOTHER OF PEACE HAS THE PREVIOUS SIX PUZZLE PIECES assembled. She has a foundation of purpose, skill, a love of work, faith, wisdom, and joy. She knows that the little tasks of her day are opportunities that inch her ever closer to the goal, and she rejoices in her progress. She is at peace with herself, her acquaintances, and the Lord. And that peace makes her a powerful mother.

34

Play by Play

"Life by the yard is hard; by the inch it's a cinch."

—President Thomas S. Monson [1]

MY FAMILY IS A LITTLE OBSESSED WITH FOOTBALL. WELL, maybe more than a little. I remember attending college football games for years before I even understood the rules. From high up in the bleachers, the players seemed to be dots of color in a line, moving forward or backward with each play. As I got into the game a little more, I learned that the offense's objective was to move ever forward until they reached the end zone. They had a wealth of resources to help them achieve their goal—years of practice, a play book, a quarterback to keep them together, and a coach directing the team from the sideline.

Sometimes the offense would gain dozens of yards in one play. These were the exciting plays, the ones fans craved. More times than not, however, they whittled away at the opponent's defense a yard—and sometimes an inch—at a time. These plays were not as fun to watch, but were still effective. Either way they were moving in the right direction. Eventually they (usually) captured their touchdown.

Inch by Inch

One of the frustrating parts about motherhood is that we can see the whole "field" of our lives at once. We can see our shortcomings, our weaknesses, and the areas where we'll just never measure up. The goal line seems so far in the distance that it can be discouraging. We long for "long pass" moments that will help us skip ahead. Sometimes we meet a trial that pushes us backward a few yards.

But we keep moving onward, trying to be content with the inches and yards that we gain. They seem small and insignificant at first. But those inches and yards add up to an eventual touchdown. Alma said, "By small and simple things are great things brought to pass; and small means in many instances doth confound the wise" (Alma 37:6).

Sometimes the game seems a bit tedious. We may be repeating some of the plays again and again. I have often joked with my children that I need some "house spray." They have hair spray to keep hair in place, so why not house spray to keep the house clean once I've cleaned it? Why can't I clean it once and have it stay that way?

Imagine if we only had to cook dinner once, or if we only had to put in one day's work at the office. What if mowing the lawn once kept it short and green forever? What if weeding the garden once kept it thriving for a lifetime? Wouldn't it be wonderful to do everything one time and be done, instead of repeating the same activities day after day?

Alas, it is not to be. But there's a reason for these seemingly mundane daily tasks. We find ourselves doing the same things, learning the same lessons in church, telling our children the same words over and over again. It can feel like we're staying in the same spot on the field. But when we occasionally look to the goal, we'll find that it is growing ever closer. Pushing through these repeated tasks and experiences, whether shoving a reluctant child out the door for church or enforcing another late-night curfew, keeps us moving in the right direction.

"Wherefore, be not weary in well-doing," the Lord tells us, "for ye are laying the foundation of a great work. And out of small things proceedeth that which is great" (Doctrine and Covenants 64:33).

As a coach would say, it helps to keep ourselves focused on the goal. President Uchtdorf called it "understanding the 'why'":

> While understanding the "what" and the "how" of the gospel is necessary, the eternal fire and majesty of the gospel springs from the "why." When we understand *why* our Heavenly Father has given us this pattern for living, when we remember *why* we committed to making it a foundational part of our lives, the gospel ceases to become a burden and, instead, becomes a joy and a delight. It becomes precious and sweet. Let us not walk the path of discipleship with our eyes on the ground, thinking only of the tasks and obligations before us. Let us not walk unaware of the beauty of the glorious earthly and spiritual landscapes that surround us. The "why" of obedience sanctifies our actions, transforming the mundane into the majestic. It *magnifies our small acts of obedience into holy acts of consecration.* [2]

There can be joy in such small tasks. We can find happiness in the game, before we even reach the "red zone" just before the goal line. Motherhood is precious and sweet when we stay focused on the "why" rather than the "what." And treasuring those precious and sweet moments won't hurt, either.

I love those "just woke up" moments when my children are snuggly and warm. I love that "ahhh" moment late at night when the kitchen is sparkly clean, the house is silent, and it's time for bed. I absolutely love those "she really *is* listening!" moments when

I hear from a teacher about a time my daughter made a good choice or said something profound at church. It is for those reasons, those three precious little blonde reasons that I tuck in every night, that I became a mother. And I can't imagine doing anything more fulfilling.

Focusing on the Goal Line

It can be hard to stay focused sometimes. We all falter occasionally when the defensive linemen of the adversary rush forward to meet us. Satan's tactic is subtle: he tries to pull us backward inch by inch. "Eat, drink, and be merry; nevertheless, fear God—he will justify in committing a little sin; yea, lie a little, take advantage of one because of his words, dig a pit for thy neighbor; there is no harm in this" (2 Nephi 28:8). But sometimes it's the hardest moments that gain us yardage in leaps and bounds. I have had some glorious trials when the Lord made Himself known to me in life-changing ways, and I knew that He really was watching and directing my efforts.

This is not a game that will be resolved in a day. It probably won't even be resolved in one great leap of faith. Sometimes it's not the tasks but the very length of the field that overwhelms us. It's the moment-to-moment decisions that are difficult. Enduring to the end truly is the hardest part about the game.

Keep moving forward. If you take nothing else from this book, take this: Whether by inches or by eighty-yard passes, keep moving forward. Your "small and simple" offerings are noticed, and they *do* make a difference.

Conclusion

Your sacrifice matters. You are making a difference, and you are doing better than you think! Sometimes it requires taking a deep breath and forcing a smile to see further than the ground-up playdough in the carpet, but your work matters. The new dent in the car's bumper or those will-this-stage-ever-end moments may make your blood boil, but you will continue to raise your children to the best of your knowledge.

You can do it. You do it every day.

Right now, each of us is in the thick of our glorious daily battles. But as the more mature ladies in Relief Society frequently tell us, these precious moments will end sooner than we think.

At the end of a long day, I like to tiptoe into my kids' bedrooms after they fall asleep and give them a kiss. Somehow, when my little angels are completely relaxed and breathing deeply, I know that I'm doing all right. I'm not a perfect mother. I think they know it too. But my kids are happy, healthy, and learning exciting new things every day. Perhaps my best really is enough.

> Keep moving forward. If you take nothing else from this book, take this: Whether by inches or by eighty-yard passes, keep moving forward. Your "small and simple" offerings are noticed, and they *do* make a difference.

We've discussed many ways to feel more peace in our busy lives. We are steadily becoming mothers of purpose, skill, work, faith, wisdom, joy, and peace. Even moms grow "line upon line, precept upon precept, here a little and there a little" (2 Nephi 28:30). It doesn't matter how fast we're going if we're headed in the right direction.

The chances are very good that you and I are already doing a great job. We are doing an important work—the "one for which all others exist."[3]

Peace of soul is a delightful consequence of getting our lives put together. If there is an area that needs tweaking, we can turn to the Lord, the ultimate Peacegiver, for help. He will not abandon us in our attempts to raise our children unto Him. And over time, as we consistently place the Lord first in our lives and teach our children to serve Him, peace will become a regular companion in our lives.

Let's fit those scattered puzzle pieces together. We are a work in progress, but at least it is *progress*. We may not see the finished product—the completed puzzle of ourselves as mothers and women of God—for a while. Perhaps not in mortality. But with our lives gently sliding into place and with a warm peace within, we will inch closer to the mothers we want to become. And surely His thoroughly tested, more mature and loving version of ourselves will be the greatest masterpiece of all.

Notes

1. Thomas S. Monson, "Believe, Obey, and Endure," *Ensign*, May 2012, 129.
2. Dieter F. Uchtdorf, "Forget Me Not," *Ensign*, November 2011, emphasis added.
3. C. S. Lewis, as quoted by Richard and Linda Eyre, *Lifebalance* (New York: Random House, 1989), 84.

The Motherhood Quiz

THINK YOU'VE SEEN IT ALL? LET'S SEE IF YOU'VE *said* IT ALL. Check the phrases you've said to your children. Then add up the scores to see where you stand:

- ___ Did you remember to wash your hands? (2 pts)
- ___ You don't have to eat all of it; just try a bite. (3 pts)
- ___ You're not leaving this room until it is clean. (3 pts)
- ___ You get what you get, and you don't throw a fit. (4 pts)
- You can't drive until you're sixteen. (2 pts)
- ___ I don't care if all your friends have them. You're not getting a cell phone until you're ____ *(insert age here)* (4 pts)
- ___ If you want shoes that cost $120, you'll have to save up for them yourself. (5 pts)
- ___ If you're that bored, come empty the dishwasher. (3 pts)
- ___ It's just a hairbrush, not an instrument of torture. (5 pts)
- ___ I thought you were going to wash your hands? (2 pts)
- ___ Wow. Um . . . when's the last time you took a shower? (4 pts)
- ___ 17,950 texts in one month? Seriously? (5 pts)
- ___ Sit up, please. We're reading scriptures. (5 pts)
- ___ Sweetheart, we don't draw on the walls. (3 pts)
- ___ Did you really punch someone at school today? (5 pts)
- ___ No, you may not watch it again. You've already watched it twice today. (2 pts)

- ___ Honey, we wear *clothes* when we go outside. (5 pts)
- ___ Didn't I tell you to wash your hands? (2 pts)
- ___ Don't lick the cat. I know she licks you, but just . . . don't. (5 pts)
- ___ What's the magic word? (2 pts)
- ___ I know it's pink, but don't you want something that's a different color? Just this once? (3 pts)
- ___ Get down from the table, please. Tables are not for standing on. (3 pts)
- ___ Time to do your homework. (2 pts)
- ___ Turn that music down. Turn down the music! I SAID, TURN IT DOWN! (5 pts)
- ___ Did you pick that gum up from off the ground? Wait—don't chew it! (3 pts)
- ___ How many times do I have to ask you to wash your hands? (2 pts)
- ___ I think your room exploded. Time for a cleaning party. (4 pts)
- ___ Are you sure you want to read that book *again*? You already have it memorized. (2 pts)
- ___ Oops, I think the video game controller disappeared. Maybe if you clean your room it will reappear. (5 pts)
- ___ Is that syrup in your hair? (3 pts)
- ___ I just mopped that floor. Here's a wet rag. Have fun! (5 pts)
- ___ Ew, sweetie. We don't eat dirt. (3 pts)
- ___ Uh, no. You are not wearing that to school, young lady. (2 pts)
- ___ You still haven't washed your hands? I give up! (5 pts)

Scores

100–118 You're Supermom! You've seen and said it all.

80–99 You're just about there. Keep up the good work!

60–79 You're not quite in the thick of things yet. Count your blessings!

0–59 Just wait. The best is yet to come.

For more fun information, facts, and resources, visit www.AuthorRebeccaRode.com.

Topic Index

Source Index

About the Author

Rebecca Rode caught the writing bug early in life, writing and illustrating stories in small journals her mother gave her at age nine. Her first published work was a personal essay about Romanian orphans, printed in Brigham Young University's literary publication, *Inscape*. She received her bachelor's degree from BYU in child development with a minor in English. Rebecca began writing for *Schooled* magazine in 2006. In 2011, she became a contributor for KSL.com, a Utah broadcasting network website, and the Deseret News in Salt Lake City. *How to Have Peace When You're Falling to Pieces* is her first book.

Rebecca enjoys traveling, eating authentic Italian gelatos, and indulging her husband's chocolate-banana shakes. Her greatest loves are her husband, Francis, their three children, and writing—in that order."

Author photo courtesy of Rachel Layton Photography.

0 26575 11701 1